Tales *from* *other* Times

Introducing
pre-twentieth century prose

by
Christine Hall
Jane Browne
Mike Hamlin

Heinemann

Heinemann Educational Publishers
Halley Court, Jordan Hill, Oxford OX2 8EJ
a division of Reed Educational and Professional Publishing Ltd

OXFORD MADRID ATHENS FLORENCE PRAGUE CHICAGO
PORTSMOUTH NH (USA) MEXICO CITY
SÃO PAULO SINGAPORE KUALA LUMPUR TOKYO MELBOURNE
AUCKLAND NAIROBI KAMPALA IBADAN GABORONE
JOHANNESBURG

First published 1996

2000 99 98 97
10 9 8 7 6 5 4 3 2

ISBN 0 435 10533 7

Designed and typeset by Moondisks Ltd, Cambridge
Cover design by Moondisks Ltd, Cambridge
Cover photo © The Bridgeman Art Gallery
Printed and bound in Great Britain by Bath Press

Introduction

Tales from other Times provides an accessible introduction to eleven pre-twentieth-century classic texts. The selections have been chosen because they have been received enthusiastically by Key Stage 3 students. They range from *Robinson Crusoe*, first published in 1719, through to *The War of the Worlds*, published in 1898.

Each of the eleven texts is featured regularly throughout the book, with key narrative moments presented in chronological order. In this way elements of an unfolding plot structure can be introduced more logically to pupils. Each extract is:

- grouped thematically, to provide opportunities for comparisons across texts
- accompanied by carefully structured activities designed to encourage a closer reading of the text under consideration, and to provide a wide range of opportunities for reflection, discussion and debate.

Students are likely to bring to the classroom some knowledge of these texts gained from film, television and other contemporary adaptations. We hope that this book will extend this knowledge and interest. Above all, we hope students will enjoy the texts and activities in this book and that they will be encouraged to explore the novels further in future years.

CHRISTINE HALL
JANE BROWNE
MIKE HAMLIN

Contents

Openings

SHERLOCK HOLMES OPENS THE CASE

BAH! HUMBUG!

GULLIVER ARRIVES IN LILLIPUT

HEATHCLIFF'S ARRIVAL

Sherlock Holmes opens the case

Sherlock Holmes is known as a world-famous detective, but he never actually lived. He is a fictional character invented by the author, Arthur Conan Doyle. He appeared in numerous mysteries, many of which have been adapted for films. Sherlock Holmes had a special talent of observing closely and finding clues which he used to make deductions about people. He then went on to solve the crime. Read the following extract, where the storyteller is Sherlock Holmes' colleague, Dr Watson…

I had no keener pleasure than in following Holmes in his professional investigations, and in admiring the rapid deductions, as swift as intuitions, and yet always founded on a logical basis, with which he unravelled the problems which were submitted to him. I rapidly threw on my clothes and was ready in a few minutes to accompany my friend down to the sitting-room. A lady dressed in black and heavily veiled, who had been sitting in the window, rose as we entered.

'Good morning, madam,' said Holmes cheerily. 'My name is Sherlock Holmes. This is my intimate friend and associate, Dr Watson, before whom you can speak as freely as before myself. Ha! I am glad to see that Mrs Hudson has had the good sense to light the fire. Pray draw up to it, and I shall order you a cup of hot coffee, for I observe that you are shivering.'

'It is not cold which makes me shiver,' said the woman in a low voice, changing her seat as requested.

'What, then?'

'It is fear, Mr Holmes. It is terror.' She raised her veil as she spoke, and we could see that she was indeed in a pitiable state of agitation, her face all drawn and grey, with restless, frightened eyes, like those of some hunted animal. Her features and figure were those of a woman of thirty, but her hair was shot with premature grey, and her expression was weary and haggard. Sherlock Holmes ran her over with one of his quick, all-comprehensive glances.

'You must not fear,' said he soothingly, bending forward and patting her forearm. 'We shall soon set matters right, I have no doubt. You have come in by train this morning, I see.'

'You know me, then?'

'No, but I observe the second half of a return ticket in the palm of your left glove. You must have started early, and yet you had a good drive in a dog-cart, along heavy roads, before you reached the station.'

The lady gave a violent start and stared in bewilderment at my companion.

'There is no mystery, my dear madam,' said he, smiling. 'The left arm of your jacket is spattered with mud in no less than seven places. The marks are perfectly fresh. There is no vehicle save a dog-cart which throws up mud in that way, and then only when you sit on the left-hand side of the driver.'

'Whatever your reasons may be, you are perfectly correct,' said she. 'I started from home before six, reached Leatherhead at twenty past, and came in by the first train to Waterloo. Sir, I can stand this strain no longer; I shall go mad if it continues. I have no one to turn to – none, save only one, who cares for me, and he, poor fellow, can be of little aid. I have heard of you, Mr Holmes; I have heard of you from Mrs Farintosh, whom you helped in the hour of her sore need. It was from her that I had your address. Oh, sir, do you not think that you could help me, too, and at least throw a little light through the dense darkness which surrounds me? At present it is out of my power to reward you for your services, but in a month or six weeks I shall be married, with the control of my own income, and then at least you shall not find me ungrateful.'

From *The Adventure of the Speckled Band* by Arthur Conan Doyle

Activities

Detective work

Sherlock Holmes noticed a number of clues about the woman in the extract. What other clues can you find?

1 Make a chart like the one below. In the first column, fill in all the clues you can find about the woman visitor.

2 In the second column, fill in the deductions you make from the clues – explain what the clues tell you about her.

Clues	What this tells us about the woman
Dressed in black.	She may be in mourning.
Heavily veiled.	
Shivering.	
Face all drawn and grey.	

Make your own deductions

Look carefully at the picture of Sherlock Holmes and his Baker Street room on the next page.

1 How much can you tell about Sherlock Holmes from the picture?

2 Make a chart similar to the one above. Working with a partner, write down all the clues about Sherlock Holmes that you can find.

3 What do the clues tell you about him? Fill in your deductions on the chart.

A new case for Sherlock Holmes

Imagine the next visitor to Sherlock Holmes' rooms. You are going to write the opening of a story describing the visitor's meeting with Sherlock Holmes. Include Holmes' deductions.

1 Think of at least six tell-tale clues about the visitor which would give Sherlock Holmes extra information and help him work out certain facts about him or her. Think about the visitor's…

- clothes
- shoes
- luggage
- something the visitor is holding.

2 Now write your opening. Remember that Sherlock Holmes will be:
- highly observant
- able to explain the conclusions he has drawn about the visitor.

Bah! Humbug!

A Christmas Carol was first published at Christmas in 1843. It was immediately a huge success, and it has remained a very popular Christmas story ever since.

Once upon a time – of all the good days in the year, on Christmas Eve – old Scrooge sat busy in his counting-house. It was cold, bleak, biting weather: foggy **withal**: and he could hear the people in the court outside, go wheezing up and down, beating their hands upon their breasts, and stamping their feet upon the pavement-stones to warm them. The city clocks had only just gone three, but it was quite dark already: it had not been light all day: and candles were flaring in the windows of the neighbouring offices, like ruddy smears upon the palpable brown air. The fog came pouring in at every chink and keyhole, and was so dense **without**, that although the court was of the narrowest, the houses opposite were mere phantoms. To see the dingy cloud come drooping down, obscuring everything, one might have thought that Nature lived hard by, and was brewing on a large scale.

The door of Scrooge's counting-house was open that he might keep his eye upon his clerk, who in a dismal little cell beyond, a sort of tank, was

withal – as well **without** – outside

copying letters. Scrooge had a very small fire, but the clerk's fire was so very much smaller that it looked like one coal. But he couldn't **replenish** it, for Scrooge kept the coal-box in his own room; and so surely as the clerk came in with the shovel, the master predicted that it would be necessary for them to part. **Wherefore** the clerk put on his white **comforter**, and tried to warm himself at the candle; in which effort, not being a man of a strong imagination, he failed.

'A merry Christmas, uncle! God save you!' cried a cheerful voice. It was the voice of Scrooge's nephew, who came upon him so quickly that this was the first **intimation** he had of his approach.

'Bah!' said Scrooge, 'Humbug!'

He had so heated himself with rapid walking in the fog and frost, this nephew of Scrooge's, that he was all in a glow; his face was ruddy and handsome; his eyes sparkled, and his breath smoked again.

'Christmas a humbug, uncle!' said Scrooge's nephew. 'You don't mean that, I am sure?'

'I do,' said Scrooge. 'Merry Christmas! What right have you to be merry? what reason have you to be merry? You're poor enough.'

'Come, then,' returned the nephew gaily. 'What right have you to be dismal? what reason have you to be morose? You're rich enough.'

Scrooge having no better answer ready on the spur of the moment, said, 'Bah!' again; and followed it up with 'Humbug.'

'Don't be cross, uncle,' said the nephew.

'What else can I be' returned the uncle, 'when I live in such a world of fools as this? Merry Christmas! Out upon merry Christmas! What's Christmas time to you but a time for paying bills, without money; a time for finding yourself a year older, and not an hour richer; a time for

---

replenish – build up   **wherefore** – for that reason   **comforter** – a long scarf
intimation – hint, sign

balancing your books and having every item in 'em through a round dozen of months presented dead against you? If I could work my will,' said Scrooge, indignantly, 'every idiot who goes about with "Merry Christmas," on his lips, should be boiled with his own pudding, and buried with a stake of holly through his heart. He should!'

From *A Christmas Carol* by Charles Dickens

Activities

Looking closely

This extract can be divided into three sections:

A a general description
B a closer focus on the scene in the office
C a conversation between Scrooge and his nephew.

1 Decide where each of these sections starts and ends.

2 Working with a partner, look at section **A** carefully.
Dickens has created the atmosphere for his story by giving details about:

* weather   • light   • sounds.

Using these as headings, make a table like the one below. Under each heading, note down the details Dickens has included in this section.

Weather	Light	Sounds
cold		
bleak		
biting		

3 In section **B** Dickens focuses on how miserly Scrooge is. These are important details for Dickens' story. Work with your partner and make a list of all the details which emphasise that Scrooge is mean.

4 In section **C** Dickens draws out the differences between Scrooge and his nephew. The contrast makes Scrooge look even meaner. Draw up a table like the one below. Work with your partner and write down as many words from the passage as you can that are associated with each of the two characters.

Scrooge	Nephew
dismal	heated

Your own writing...

A *Christmas Carol* is about the main character, Scrooge, learning to change. You are going to write the opening few paragraphs to a story, using a plan like Charles Dickens used.

I Think about the **opening** to your story, which should be about one of the following:
- a very bad-tempered, angry person who is always losing his or her temper
- a very selfish person who thinks about no one but him- or herself.

2 Planning section A:

a Pick a name for your character that sounds like a bad-tempered or selfish person.

b Think about the details you might use in your opening paragraph, for example:
- the weather
- the time of day
- where it is taking place ('the scene').

c Now think about how to describe these details:
- weather conditions that fit your character (blazing hot weather for an angry person? cold, icy weather for a selfish one?)
- the time of day – this will affect what light and colour there is in your paragraph
- sounds that fit in well with the scene.

3 Planning section B:

   a Decide on a setting within the main scene which will show up the strong characteristics of your character. You can use this to emphasise your character's bad temper or selfishness.

   b Make a list of the details you will include in your description.

4 Planning section C:

   a Introduce a new character who holds a conversation with your main character. Choose someone who is completely different – either very good-tempered or very unselfish.

   b Work out an outline conversation that will emphasise the main character's personality.

5 Now write your opening:
- write it in three parts, using your plan
- keep it short
- make sure that everything in it adds to what the reader knows about your character's bad temper or selfishness.

6 Choose a partner, and each read your own story aloud to the other. When you are listening to your partner's story, think about why he or she has included each of the details – and if you are not sure, ask.

Gulliver arrives in Lilliput

Lemuel Gulliver had set sail from Bristol in 1699 aboard the good ship *Antelope*. Several months later, as they were travelling through the South Seas, they hit a violent storm. The ship ran aground and many of the crew were killed, but somehow Gulliver managed to escape. As probably the sole survivor, he was eventually washed up on the shore of an unknown island. His adventures in Lilliput were about to begin…

I … advanced forward near half a mile, but could not discover any signs of houses or inhabitants; at least I was in so weak a condition, that I did not observe them. I was extremely tired, and with that, and the heat of the weather, and about half a pint of brandy that I drank as I left the ship, I found myself much inclined to sleep. I lay down on the grass, which was very short and soft, where I slept sounder than ever I remember to have done in my life, and as I reckoned, above nine hours; for when I awaked, it was just daylight. I attempted to rise, but was not able to stir: for as I happened to lie on my back, I found my arms and legs were strongly fastened on each side to the ground; and my hair, which was long and thick, tied down in the same manner. I likewise felt several slender **ligatures** across my body, from my armpits to my thighs. I could only look upwards, the sun began to grow hot, and the light offended mine eyes. I heard a confused noise about me, but in the posture I lay, could see nothing except the sky. In a little time I felt something alive moving on my left leg, which advancing gently forward over my breast, came almost up to my chin; when bending mine eyes downwards as much as I could, I perceived it to be a human creature not six inches high, with a bow and arrow in his hands, and a quiver at his back. In the meantime, I felt at least forty more of the same kind (as I **conjectured**) following the first. I was in the utmost astonishment, and roared so loud, that they all ran back in a fright; and some of them, as I was afterwards told, were hurt with the falls they got by leaping from my sides upon the ground. However, they soon returned, and one of them, who ventured so far as to get a full sight of my face, lifting up

ligatures – straps, ties, bonds **conjectured** – guessed

his hands and eyes by way of admiration, cried out in a shrill, but distinct voice, *Hekinah degul*: the others repeated the same words several times, but I then knew not what they meant. I lay all this while, as the reader may believe, in great uneasiness…

From *Gulliver's Travels* by Jonathan Swift

Hekinah degul – words from an imaginary language

Activities

Captions

As readers, we build up a picture of what is happening to Gulliver through a series of descriptions. The key moments in this series of events have been drawn for you on the following pages as frames in a simple picture story.

1 Read through the passage, linking the picture frames to the events as they unfold.

2 Using your own words, write short but accurate commentaries to go with each of the frames. For example, the commentary on the first story frame might be:

'I stumbled on for about half a mile, seeing no houses or inhabitants. I felt weak and tired as it was very hot in the sun.'

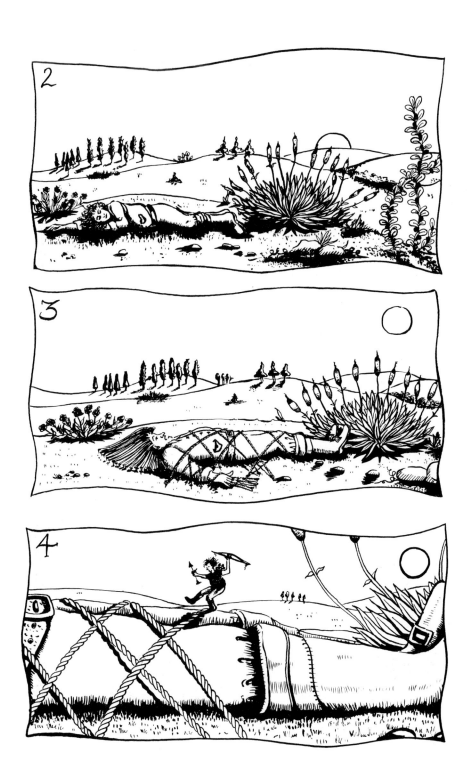

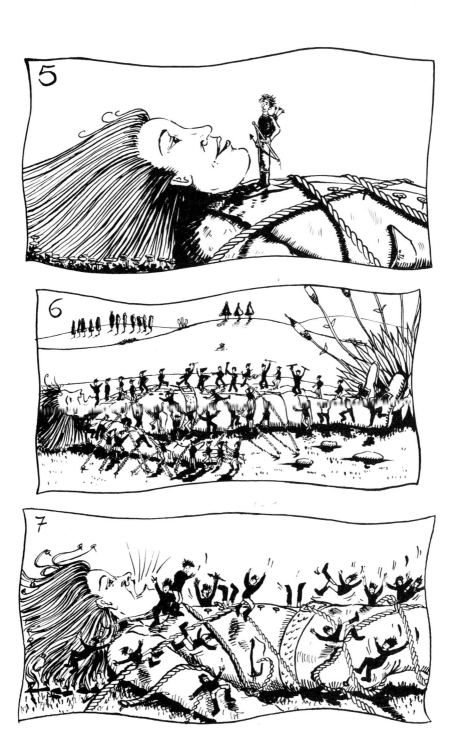

Predictions

Gulliver describes his first impressions of the island from his own, personal point of view: 'I advanced forward... I was in so weak a condition...'. This is known as **first person story telling**.

'He advanced forward... He was in so weak a condition...' is known as **third person story telling**.

From what you have discovered about the opening of this story, predict how it might develop from here.

1 Write as a **third person story**. Take it up to a point where Gulliver is somehow introduced to the leader of this strange island community.

2 Continue to write as a **first person story**, as if you were Gulliver. You will need to think about what might happen to him after he has met the leader:
   • what sort of leader might the inhabitants have?
   • will the leader talk directly to Gulliver, or will they need an interpreter?
   • how will the inhabitants treat Gulliver – will he seem strange to them?
   • will they be frightened or friendly?

This is the first time we meet Heathcliff, who is one of the main characters in *Wuthering Heights*. As you can see, he gets a very hostile reception. The story is told by Nelly, a servant.

We crowded round, and, over Miss Cathy's head, I had a peep at a dirty, ragged, black-haired child; big enough both to walk and talk – indeed, its face looked older than Catherine's – yet, when it was set on its feet, it only stared round, and repeated over and over again some gibberish that nobody could understand. I was frightened, and Mrs Earnshaw was ready to fling it out of doors: she did fly up – asking how he could fashion to bring that gipsy brat into the house, when they had their own bairns to feed, and fend for? What he meant to do with it, and whether he were mad?

The master tried to explain the matter; but he was really half dead with fatigue, and all that I could make out, amongst her scolding, was a tale of his seeing it starving, and houseless, and as good as dumb in the streets of Liverpool where he picked it up and inquired for its owner – Not a soul knew to whom it belonged, he said, and his money and time, being both limited, he thought it better to take it home with him, at once, than run into vain expenses there; because he was determined he would not leave it as he found it.

Well, the conclusion was that my mistress grumbled herself calm; and Mr Earnshaw told me to wash it, and give it clean things, and let it sleep with the children.

Hindley and Cathy contented themselves with looking and listening till peace was restored; then, both began searching their father's pockets for the presents he had promised them. The former was a boy of fourteen, but when he drew out what had been a fiddle, crushed to morsels in the greatcoat, he blubbered aloud, and Cathy, when she learnt the master had lost her whip in attending on the stranger, showed her humour by grinning and spitting at the stupid little thing, earning for her pains a sound blow from her father to teach her cleaner manners.

They entirely refused to have it in bed with them, or even in their room, and I had no more sense, so, I put it on the landing of the stairs, hoping it might be gone on the morrow. By chance, or else attracted by hearing his voice, it crept to Mr Earnshaw's door, and there he found it on quitting his chamber. Inquiries were made as to how it got there; I was obliged to confess, and in recompense for my cowardice and inhumanity was sent out of the house.

This was Heathcliff's first introduction to the family; on coming back a few days afterwards, for I did not consider my banishment perpetual, I found they had christened him 'Heathcliff'; it was the name of a son who died in childhood, and it has served him ever since, both for Christian and surname.

From *Wuthering Heights* by Emily Brontë

Activities

Meeting Heathcliff

1 Discuss these questions with a partner:

a What does the passage tell us about Heathcliff's past life?

b How does each of the following characters react to Heathcliff?
- Mrs Earnshaw
- Mr Earnshaw
- Hindley
- Cathy
- Nelly.

2 Get into groups of six and choose one of the characters each. Act out the story in the passage above. Make sure that you react as your character does in Nelly's description of the scene.

3 In the same groups, spend five minutes interviewing Heathcliff. How did it feel to arrive in the family in this way?

Heathcliff's point of view

4 Write an account of this episode from Heathcliff's point of view. Start your
account from where Mr Earnshaw sets Heathcliff down on his feet for the family
to see him.

- Remember that he has been bundled up in Mr Earnshaw's arms on his journey
  from Liverpool to the Yorkshire Moors.
- Think about how Heathcliff would react to being in the house after living rough.
  Show that reaction in your writing.
- Show the reactions of each of the characters.
- Keep the detail of your account true to the detail in the original.

Introducing character

EBENEZER SCROOGE

MR D'URBERVILLE

SILAS MARNER

CATHY EARNSHAW

Ebenezer Scrooge

Scrooge is perhaps the most well-known of all characters from novels by Charles Dickens. *A Christmas Carol* has been dramatised many times on stage and on television and there are many versions of the story for young children.

What does the word 'scrooge' mean to you? What does it mean if you call someone 'a scrooge'? What image do you have of Charles Dickens' character, Scrooge? Read the extract below.

Oh! but he was a tight-fisted hand at the **grindstone**, Scrooge! A squeezing, wrenching, grasping, scraping, clutching, **covetous** old sinner! Hard and sharp as flint, from which no steel had ever struck out generous fire; secret, and self-contained, and solitary as an oyster. The cold within him froze his old features, nipped his pointed nose, shrivelled his cheek, stiffened his **gait**; made his eyes red, his thin lips blue; and spoke out shrewdly in his grating voice. A frosty **rime** was on his head, and on his eyebrows, and his wiry chin. He carried his own low temperature always about with him; he iced his office in the **dog-days**; and didn't thaw it one degree at Christmas.

External heat and cold had little influence on Scrooge. No warmth could warm, nor wintry weather chill him. No wind that blew was bitterer than he, no falling snow was more intent upon its purpose, no pelting rain less open to entreaty. Foul weather didn't know where to have him. The heaviest rain, and snow, and hail, and sleet, could boast of the advantage over him in only one respect. They often 'came down' handsomely, and Scrooge never did.

grindstone – revolving disc used for sharpening or grinding things
covetous – desiring things, especially things belonging to other people
gait – way of walking   **rime** – frost   **dog-days** – hottest days

Nobody ever stopped him in the street to say, with gladsome looks, 'My dear Scrooge, how are you? When will you come to see me?' No beggars implored him to **bestow** a **trifle**, no children asked him what it was o'clock, no man or woman ever once in all his life inquired the way to such and such a place, of Scrooge. Even the blindmen's dogs appeared to know him; and when they saw him coming on, would tug their owners into doorways and up courts; and then would wag their tails as though they said, 'no eye at all is better than an evil eye, dark master!'

But what did Scrooge care? It was the very thing he liked. To edge his way along the crowded paths of life, warning all human sympathy to keep its distance, was what the knowing ones call 'nuts' to Scrooge.

From *A Christmas Carol* by Charles Dickens

bestow – give **trifle** – very small amount

Activities

I **Paragraph one** of the extract uses many words and phrases to describe the character of Scrooge. Make a table like the one below.

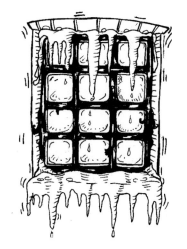

a Write down all the words linked to *hardness* in column I and all the words linked to *coldness* in column 2.

b In column 3, make a list of other descriptive words or phrases about Scrooge. (If you are not sure what a word means, look it up in the dictionary.) What do each of *these* words or phrases suggest to you about Scrooge's character?

Hardness	Coldness	Other descriptive words or phrases
grindstone	froze	squeezing wrenching

2 **Paragraph two** of the extract considers the *lack* of influence that weather and the elements have on Scrooge.

    a What point about Scrooge do you think is being made here?

    b What sort of a character would be completely indifferent to his or her physical surroundings?

3 **Paragraphs three and four** continue by discussing the way people in general relate, or fail to relate, to Scrooge.

    a What point do you think is being made about Scrooge here?

    b Why might the behaviour of *other* people tell us something about the character of Scrooge himself?

4 Early in the extract Dickens describes Scrooge as being as 'self-contained, and solitary as an oyster'. Do you think this comparison is an accurate one? Give some examples of why you agree or disagree.

Scrooge in reverse!

Write a character description for someone with a personality which is exactly the opposite of Ebenezer Scrooge.

I Give your character a suitable name – for example, Ms Generosity Lovepenny or Mr Hand-Shake Warmheart.

2 Write three or four paragraphs of concentrated description. You have seen how Dickens developed Scrooge's character paragraph by paragraph, as outlined above. Follow the same pattern for developing your character. Your paragraphs should emphasise:
- words connected to *softness* and *warmth* for paragraph one
- a *sensitivity* to weather and the natural environment for paragraph two
- an *awareness* and *involvement* with other human beings for paragraphs three and four.

You should end up with a powerful and entertaining description of someone who is the exact opposite of Ebenezer Scrooge – a Scrooge in reverse!

Meeting Mr d'Urberville

Tess of the d'Urbervilles tells the story of Tess, an innocent young country girl whose life takes a downward turn after her involvement with Alec d'Urberville.

Tess still stood hesitating like a bather about to make his plunge, hardly knowing whether to retreat or to persevere, when a figure came forth from the dark triangular door of the tent. It was that of a tall young man, smoking.

He had an almost swarthy complexion, with full lips, badly moulded, though red and smooth, above which was a well-groomed black moustache with curled points, though his age could not be more than three- or four-and-twenty. Despite the touches of **barbarism** in his **contours**, there was a singular force in the gentleman's face, and in his bold rolling eye.

barbarism – wildness
contours – face, appearance

> 'Well, my Beauty, what can I do for you?' said he, coming forward. And perceiving that she stood quite **confounded**: 'Never mind me. I am Mr d'Urberville. Have you come to see me or my mother?'

From *Tess of the d'Urbervilles* by Thomas Hardy

confounded – confused, perplexed

Activities

Impressions about characters

1 How can we tell that Tess is rather nervous about the meeting?

2 We realise that Thomas Hardy wanted to make Alec d'Urberville appear attractive, but rather dangerous.

    a To help you see how Hardy does this, make a list of those points which tell you Alec d'Urberville is a rogue – a 'baddie'.

    b How do you respond to some of those descriptions which Hardy uses?

Introducing a character

3 In a paragraph of just over one hundred words, Thomas Hardy has given the reader a clear impression of Alec d'Urberville as something of a scoundrel. Try your hand at introducing a dangerous or untrustworthy character. Write about four sentences of description followed by an opening line of direct speech.

    a Choose your character. It might be:
- a spoiled child
- an obsessive gambler
- a disruptive pupil
- an unfair teacher
- a drug dealer
- a confidence trickster...

    b Give a description of the character's outward appearance which is designed to make the reader feel mistrustful.

Silas and his money

Silas Marner has lived in Raveloe for fifteen years, spending all his days at his loom. Weaving and money fill his thoughts, day and night.

This is the history of Silas Marner until the fifteenth year after he came to Raveloe. The **livelong** day he sat in his loom, his ear filled with its monotony, his eyes bent close down on the slow growth of sameness in the

livelong – whole

brownish web, his muscles moving with such even repetition that their pause seemed almost as much a constraint as the holding of his breath. But at night came his **revelry**: at night he closed his shutters, and made fast his doors, and drew out his gold. Long ago the heap of coins had become too large for the iron pot to hold them, and he had made for them two thick leather bags, which wasted no room in their resting-place, but lent themselves flexibly to every corner. How the guineas shone as they came pouring out of the dark leather mouths! The silver bore no large proportion in amount to the gold, because the long pieces of linen which formed his chief work were always partly paid for in gold, and out of the silver he supplied his own bodily wants, choosing always the shillings and sixpences to spend in this way. He loved the guineas best, but he would not change the silver – the crowns and half-crowns that were his own earnings, **begotten** by his labour; he loved them all. He spread them out in heaps and bathed his hands in them; he counted them and set them up in regular piles, and felt their rounded outline between his thumb and fingers, and thought fondly of the guineas that were only half-earned by the work in his loom, as if they had been unborn children – thought of the guineas that were coming slowly through the coming years, through all his life, which spread far away before him, the end quite hidden by countless days of weaving. No wonder his thoughts were still with his loom and his money when he made his journeys through the fields and the lanes to fetch and carry home his work, so that his steps never wandered to the hedge-banks and the lane-side in search of the once familiar herbs: these too belonged to the past, from which his life had shrunk away, like a rivulet that has sunk far down from the grassy fringe of its old breadth into a little shivering thread that cuts a groove for itself in the barren sand.

From *Silas Marner* by George Eliot

---

revelry – entertainment   **begotten** – created, the result of

Activities

Creating atmosphere

This description of Silas Marner's life is divided into two parts – one about the *day-time* and one about the *night-time*.

1 Look at the part describing the day-time.

    a How does George Eliot make Silas' days seem slow and boring?

    b Pick out the words and phrases which give this impression.

2 Now look at the description of Silas' evenings.

    a Which words and phrases give the impression of Silas' excitement?

    b Why is this section much longer than the description of the day?

3 Silas is a man obsessed with money.

    a What images does the writer use to show how important money is to him?

    b Why does the writer choose these images?

    c What do these images make *you* feel about Silas?

Days and nights

4 Think about some other obsessions which people have – e.g. gambling, playing computer games or surfing the Internet. Write a short story about a character with an obsession.

- remember that, although the reason can't be easily explained to other people, an obsession is something that will *totally absorb* the character
- help the reader to understand how your character feels
- use the same model for your writing as in the extract:

    Day: briefly describe something suitable but boring that fills your character's day

    Night: the obsession takes over and …

Use what you have learned from George Eliot's writing to help you write more effectively.

'A wild, wick slip'

This part of *Wuthering Heights* is being told by Nelly, one of the servants. It describes the character of Cathy as a girl, and her rather difficult relationship with her father.

She had ways with her such as I never saw a child take up before; and she put all of us past our patience fifty times and oftener in a day; from the hour she came downstairs, till the hour she went to bed, we had not a moment's security that she wouldn't be in mischief. Her spirits were always at high-water mark, her tongue always going – singing, laughing, and plaguing everybody who would not do the same. A wild, wick slip she was – but she had the bonniest eye, and sweetest smile, and lightest foot in the parish; and, after all, I believe she meant no harm; for when once she made you cry in good earnest, it seldom happened that she would not keep you company; and oblige you to be quiet that you might comfort her.

She was much too fond of Heathcliff. The greatest punishment we could invent for her was to keep her separate from him: yet she got chided more than any of us on his account.

In play, she liked, exceedingly, to act the little mistress; using her hands freely, and commanding her companions: she did so to me, but I would not bear slapping, and ordering; and so I let her know.

Now, Mr Earnshaw did not understand jokes from his children: he had always been strict and grave with them; and Catherine, on her part, had no idea why her father should be crosser and less patient in his ailing condition, than he was in his prime.

His peevish reproofs wakened in her a naughty delight to provoke him; she was never so happy as when we were all scolding her at once, and she defying us with her bold, saucy look, and her ready words; turning Joseph's religious curses into ridicule, baiting me, and doing just what her father hated most, showing how her pretended insolence, which he thought real, had more power over Heathcliff than his kindness. How the boy would do *her* bidding in anything, and *his* only when it suited his own inclination.

After behaving as badly as possible all day, she sometimes came fondling to make it up at night.

'Nay, Cathy,' the old man would say, 'I cannot love thee; thou'rt worse than thy brother. Go, say thy prayers, child, and ask God's pardon. I doubt thy mother and I must rue that we ever reared thee!'

That made her cry, at first; and then, being repulsed continually hardened her, and she laughed if I told her to say she was sorry for her faults, and beg to be forgiven.

But the hour came, at last, that ended Mr Earnshaw's troubles on earth. He died quietly in his chair one October evening, seated by the fireside.

A high wind blustered round the house, and roared in the chimney: it sounded wild and stormy, yet it was not cold, and we were all together – I, a little removed from the hearth, busy at my knitting, and Joseph reading his Bible near the table (for the servants generally sat in the house then, after their work was done). Miss Cathy had been sick, and that made her still; she leant against her father's knee, and Heathcliff was lying on the floor with his head in her lap.

I remember the master, before he fell into a doze, stroking her bonny hair – it pleased him rarely to see her gentle – and saying –

'Why canst thou not always be a good lass, Cathy?'

And she turned her face up to his, and laughed, and answered –

'Why cannot you always be a good man, father?'

But as soon as she saw him vexed again, she kissed his hand, and said she would sing him to sleep. She began singing very low, till his fingers dropped from hers, and his head sank on his breast. Then I told her to hush, and not stir, for fear she should wake him. We all kept as mute as mice a full half hour, and should have done longer, only Joseph, having finished his chapter, got up and said that he must rouse the master for prayers and bed. He stepped forward, and called him by name, and touched his shoulder, but he would not move – so he took the candle and looked at him.

I thought there was something wrong as he set down the light; and seizing the children each by an arm, whispered them to '**frame** upstairs, and make little din – they might pray alone that evening – he had summut to do.'

'I shall bid father good-night first,' said Catherine, putting her arms round his neck before we could hinder her.

The poor thing discovered her loss directly – she screamed out –

'Oh, he's dead, Heathcliff! he's dead!'

And they both set up a heart-breaking cry.

I joined my wail to theirs, loud and bitter; but Joseph asked what we could be thinking of to roar in that way over a saint in heaven.

frame – go

He told me to put on my cloak and run to Gimmerton for the doctor and the parson. I could not guess the use that either would be of, then. However, I went, through wind and rain, and brought one, the doctor, back with me; the other said he would come in the morning.

Leaving Joseph to explain matters, I ran to the children's room; their door was ajar, I saw they had never laid down, though it was past midnight; but they were calmer, and did not need me to console them. The little souls were comforting each other with better thoughts than I could have hit on; no parson in the world ever pictured heaven so beautifully as they did, in their innocent talk; and, while I sobbed, and listened, I could not help wishing we were all there safe together.

From *Wuthering Heights* by Emily Brontë

Activities

Cathy's character

1 Make a table like the one below. Read through the passage and pick out all the points you can which describe Cathy's character, listing them in column 1. Leave a few lines between each point.

2 Opposite each aspect of Cathy's character note down the evidence for that point in column 2. Much will come from Nelly's view of Cathy.

Cathy's character	How do we know this?
She was very fond of Heathcliff.	1 Nelly says so. 2 When she finds her father is dead, she turns to Heathcliff first.

Predictions

1 Think about what you have learned from this passage. Working with a partner, try to predict six things which might happen to these characters in the rest of *Wuthering Heights*. They might happen immediately, or some years in the future – or both. Write down your predictions, and your reasons for them.

2 Compare your ideas with other people's. Did similar reasons lead to similar predictions, or different ones?

Describing people, places and things

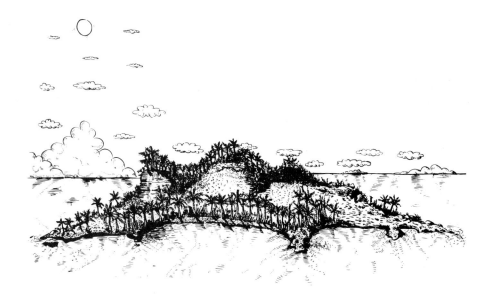

A sketch of Robinson Crusoe

Robinson Crusoe tells the story of how a sailor was washed up on a desert island and lived there for twenty-eight years – most of it alone. He made his clothes as best he could from anything which was to hand. In the following passage Daniel Defoe gives a description of the outfit Robinson Crusoe made for himself. The book was first published in 1719 and the extract is in the language of the early eighteenth century.

I had a great high shapeless cap, made of a goat's skin, with a flap hanging down behind, as well to keep the sun from me, as to shoot the rain off from running into my neck; nothing being so hurtful in these climates as the rain upon flesh, under the clothes.

I had a short jacket of goat-skin, the skirts coming down to about the middle of my thighs; and a pair of open-kneed breeches of the same. The breeches were made of the skin of an old he-goat, whose hair hung down such a length on either side, that, like pantaloons, it reached to the middle of my legs. Stockings and shoes I had none, but had made

me a pair of somethings, I scarce know what to call them, like **buskins**, to flap over my legs, and lace on either side like **spatterdashes**; but of a most barbarous shape, as indeed were all the rest of my clothes.

I had on a broad belt of goat's skin dried, which I drew together with two thongs of the same, instead of buckles; and in a kind of a **frog** on either side of this, instead of a sword and a dagger, hung a little saw and a hatchet, one on one side, one on the other. I had another belt, not so broad, and fastened in the same manner, which hung over my shoulder; and at the end of it, under my left arm, hung two pouches, both made of goat's skin too; in one of which I hung my powder, in the other my shot. At my back I carried my basket, on my shoulder my gun, and over my head a great clumsy ugly goat-skin umbrella, but which, after all, was the most necessary thing I had about me, next to my gun.

From *Robinson Crusoe* by Daniel Defoe

buskins – high boots   **spatterdashes** – leggings to protect stockings from mud
frog – an attachment to a belt, to support a sword

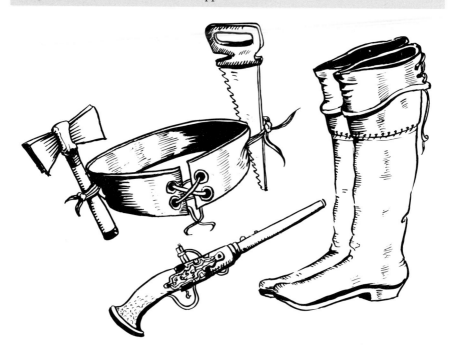

Activities

Investigating the text

1 Read the passage carefully. Using the information contained there, draw a simple outline figure of Robinson Crusoe showing the clothes he is wearing.

2 Label the clothes, making use of quotations from the passage to describe them, e.g. 'belt (dried goat's skin)'.

Following on

1 Imagine a character who is a victim of fashion. He or she will be wearing all the latest trends, whether it is from the 1970s, the 1980s or the present day.

2 Write a 'top to toe' description of your character. Make your description detailed enough so that anyone reading it can imagine *exactly* what he or she looks like. You will need to be precise in your description of garment, fabric and style, e.g.

'the trousers, made from purple crushed velvet, are high-waisted, with patch pockets and 90-centimetre flares.'

Have fun working out an unusual, even outrageous outfit. Make your language as accurate and precise as the character would be in their choice of clothes.

The Cratchits' Christmas dinner

Bob Cratchit works for Scrooge as his clerk. A ghost, the Ghost of Christmas Present, has appeared to Scrooge and is showing him the Cratchit family at home, enjoying their Christmas dinner. They are a happy family though poor.

Mrs Cratchit made the gravy (ready beforehand in a little saucepan) hissing hot; Master Peter mashed the potatoes with incredible vigour; Miss Belinda sweetened up the apple-sauce; Martha dusted the hot plates; Bob took Tiny Tim beside him in a tiny corner at the table; the two young Cratchits set chairs for everybody, not forgetting themselves, and mounting guard upon their posts, crammed spoons into their mouths, lest they should shriek for goose before their turn came to be helped. At last the dishes were set on, and grace was said. It was succeeded by a breathless pause, as Mrs Cratchit, looking slowly all along the carving-knife, prepared to plunge it in the breast; but when she did, and when the long expected gush of stuffing issued forth, one murmur of delight arose all round the board, and even Tiny Tim, excited by the two young Cratchits, beat on the table with the handle of his knife, and feebly cried Hurrah!

There never was such a goose. Bob said he didn't believe there ever was such a goose cooked. Its tenderness and flavour, size and cheapness, were the themes of universal admiration. Eked out by the apple-sauce

and mashed potatoes, it was a sufficient dinner for the whole family; indeed, as Mrs Cratchit said with great delight (surveying one small atom of a bone upon the dish), they hadn't ate it all at last! Yet every one had had enough, and the youngest Cratchits in particular, were steeped in sage and onion to the eyebrows! But now, the plates being changed by Miss Belinda, Mrs Cratchit left the room alone – too nervous to bear witnesses – to take the pudding up, and bring it in.

Suppose it should not be done enough! Suppose it should break in turning out! Suppose somebody should have got over the wall of the back-yard, and stolen it, while they were merry with the goose: a supposition at which the two young Cratchits became livid! All sorts of horrors were supposed.

Hallo! A great deal of steam! The pudding was out of the copper. A smell like a washing-day! That was the cloth. A smell like an eating-house, and a pastry cook's next door to each other, with a laundress's

next door to that! That was the pudding. In half a minute Mrs Cratchit entered: flushed, but smiling proudly: with the pudding, like a speckled cannon-ball, so hard and firm, blazing in half of half-a-quartern of ignited brandy, and **bedight** with Christmas holly stuck into the top.

Oh, a wonderful pudding! Bob Cratchit said, and calmly too, that he regarded it as the greatest success achieved by Mrs Cratchit since their marriage. Mrs Cratchit said that now the weight was off her mind, she would confess she had had her doubts about the quantity of flour. Everybody had something to say about it, but nobody said or thought it was at all a small pudding for a large family. It would have been flat heresy to do so. Any Cratchit would have blushed to hint at such a thing.

At last the dinner was all done, the cloth was cleared, the hearth swept, and the fire made up. The compound in the jug being tasted, and considered perfect, apples and oranges were put upon the table, and a shovel-full of chestnuts on the fire. Then all the Cratchit family drew round the hearth, in what Bob Cratchit called a circle, meaning half a one; and at Bob Cratchit's elbow stood the family display of glass; two tumblers, and a custard-cup without a handle.

These held the hot stuff from the jug, however, as well as golden goblets would have done; and Bob served it out with beaming looks, while the chestnuts on the fire sputtered and crackled noisily. Then Bob proposed:

'A Merry Christmas to us all, my dears. God bless us!'

Which all the family re-echoed.

'God bless us every one!' said Tiny Tim, the last of all.

He sat very close to his father's side, upon his little stool. Bob held his withered little hand in his, as if he loved the child, and wished to keep him by his side, and dreaded that he might be taken from him.

bedight – decorated

'Spirit,' said Scrooge, with an interest he had never felt before, 'tell me if Tiny Tim will live.'

'I see a vacant seat,' replied the Ghost, 'in the poor chimney corner, and a crutch without an owner, carefully preserved. If these shadows remain unaltered by the Future, the child will die.'

From *A Christmas Carol* by Charles Dickens

Activities

The episodes

I Read through the passage and find short quotations which describe the atmosphere in the Cratchits' home in each of the paragraphs below:

a The first paragraph.

b The paragraph beginning 'Oh, a wonderful pudding!'

c The paragraph beginning 'At last the dinner was all done...'

d The paragraph beginning 'He sat very close to his father's side...'

Playscript

2 Write a version of the scene as a play. You should base your script very closely on the original text. Where possible, use the same details and even the same language.

a You will need these characters:

- Bob Cratchit
- Mrs Cratchit
- Peter
- Belinda
- Martha
- Tiny Tim
- The Ghost
- Scrooge

b You could start with these lines:

Mrs Cratchit: I've made the gravy already. There! It's good and hot now!

Peter: I'll mash the potatoes, Mother!

(*Grabbing the pan and beginning to mash with great vigour*)

School breakfast

Jane Eyre, an orphan, has been sent away to a boarding school called Lowood. She arrives at night-time; the passage describes what happens to her the next morning.

When I again unclosed my eyes, a loud bell was ringing; the girls were up and dressing; day had not yet begun to dawn, and a rushlight or two burnt in the room. I too rose reluctantly; it was bitter cold, and I dressed as well as I could for shivering, and washed when there was a basin at liberty, which did not occur soon, as there was but one basin to six girls, on the stands down the middle of the room. Again the bell rang: all formed in file, two and two, and in that order descended the stairs and entered the cold and dimly-lit schoolroom: here prayers were read by Miss Miller; afterwards she called out –

'Form classes!'

A great tumult succeeded for some minutes, during which Miss Miller repeatedly exclaimed, 'Silence!' and 'Order!' When it subsided, I saw them all drawn up in four semicircles, before four chairs, placed at the four tables: all held books in their hands, and a great book, like a Bible, lay on each table, before the vacant seat. A pause of some seconds succeeded, filled up by the low, vague hum of numbers; Miss Miller walked from class to class, hushing this indefinite sound. ➡

A distant bell tinkled: immediately three ladies entered the room, each walked to a table and took her seat; Miss Miller assumed the fourth vacant chair, which was that nearest the door, and around which the smallest of the children were assembled: to this inferior class I was called, and placed at the bottom of it.

Business now began: the day's Collect was repeated, then certain texts of Scripture were said, and to these succeeded a protracted reading of chapters in the Bible, which lasted an hour. By the time that exercise was terminated, day had fully dawned. The **indefatigable** bell now sounded for the fourth time: the classes were marshalled and marched into another room to breakfast. How glad I was to behold a prospect of getting something to eat! I was now nearly sick from **inanition**, having taken so little the day before.

The **refectory** was a great, low-ceiled, gloomy room; on two long tables smoked basins of something hot, which, however, to my dismay, sent forth an odour far from inviting, I saw a universal **manifestation** of discontent when the fumes of the repast met the nostrils of those destined to swallow it; from the **van** of the procession, the tall girls of the first class, rose the whispered words –

'Disgusting! The porridge is burnt again!'

'Silence!' ejaculated a voice; not that of Miss Miller, but one of the upper teachers, a little dark personage, smartly dressed, but of somewhat morose aspect, who installed herself at the top of one table, while a more buxom lady presided at the other. I looked in vain for her I had first seen the night before; she was not visible. Miss Miller occupied the foot of the table where I sat; and a strange foreign-looking, elderly lady, the French teacher, as I afterwards found, took the corresponding seat at the other board. A long grace was said, and a hymn sung; then a servant brought in some tea for the teachers, and the meal began.

---

indefatigable – untiring **inanition** – lack of nourishment
refectory – dining-room **manifestation** – expression **van** – front

Ravenous, and now very faint, I devoured a spoonful or two of my portion without thinking of its taste, but the first edge of hunger blunted, I perceived I had got in hand a nauseous mess – burnt porridge is almost as bad as rotten potatoes; famine itself soon sickens over it. The spoons were moved slowly: I saw each girl taste her food and try to swallow it; but in most cases the effort was soon relinquished. Breakfast was over, and none had breakfasted.

From *Jane Eyre* by Charlotte Brontë

Activities

School rules

I Use the passage to work out some of the school rules at Lowood. It is clear that everything must be done in a strict order and at a precise time. Write the entry from getting up in the morning until breakfast. Put in suitable times; the first few entries have been done to start you off.

Lowood School order of the day	
5 a.m.	Bell rings for waking up.
5.05	All girls to be properly dressed.
5.10 – 5.20	Wash in cold water.

Writing home

2 Imagine that you are one of the girls at Lowood School. You have watched Jane Eyre during her first school breakfast. Write a letter to a cousin of your own age, describing Jane's reactions and your own feelings about being at Lowood. When you describe your feelings, try to explain *why* you feel as you do.

The cylinder opens

Strange sightings have been reported around the London area and rumours are spreading that visitors from outer space have been landing.

A crowd has now gathered at one of these sightings, expecting to be surprised …

I saw a young man, a shop assistant in Woking I believe he was, standing on the cylinder and trying to scramble out of the hole again. The crowd had pushed him in.

The end of the cylinder was being screwed out from within. Nearly two feet of shining screw projected. Somebody blundered against me, and I narrowly missed being pitched on to the top of the screw. I turned, and as I did so the screw must have come out, for the lid of the cylinder fell upon the gravel with a ringing concussion. I stuck my elbow into the person behind me, and turned my head towards the Thing again. For a moment that circular cavity seemed perfectly black. I had the sunset in my eyes.

I think everyone expected to see a man emerge – possibly something a little unlike us terrestrial men, but in all essentials a man. I know I did. But, looking, I presently saw something stirring within the shadow: greyish billowy movements, one above another, and then two luminous discs – like eyes. Then something resembling a little grey snake, about the thickness of a walking-stick, coiled up out of the writhing middle, and wriggled in the air towards me – and then another.

A sudden chill came over me. There was a loud shriek from a woman behind. I half turned, keeping my eyes fixed upon the cylinder still, from which other tentacles were now projecting, and began pushing my way back from the edge of the pit. I saw astonishment giving place to horror on the faces of the people about me. I heard inarticulate exclamations on all sides. There was a general movement backwards. I saw the shopman struggling still on the edge of the pit. I found myself alone, and saw the people on the other side of the pit running off... I looked again at the cylinder, and ungovernable terror gripped me. I stood petrified and staring.

A big greyish rounded bulk, the size, perhaps, of a bear, was rising slowly and painfully out of the cylinder. As it bulged up and caught the light, it glistened like wet leather.

Two large dark-coloured eyes were regarding me steadfastly. The mass that framed them, the head of the thing, was rounded, and had, one might say, a face. There was a mouth under the eyes, the lipless brim of which quivered and panted, and dropped saliva. The whole creature heaved and pulsated convulsively. A lank **tentacular appendage** gripped the edge of the cylinder, another swayed in the air.

Those who have never seen a living Martian can scarcely imagine the strange horror of its appearance. The peculiar V-shaped mouth with its pointed upper lip, the absence of brow ridges, the absence of a chin beneath the wedge-like lower lip, the incessant quivering of this mouth, the **Gorgon** groups of tentacles, the tumultuous breathing of the lungs

---

tentacular appendage – a tentacle-like limb or attachment
Gorgon – snake-like

in a strange atmosphere, the evident heaviness and painfulness of movement due to the greater gravitational energy of the earth – above all, the extraordinary intensity of the immense eyes – were at once, vital, intense, inhuman, crippled and monstrous. There was something fungoid in the oily brown skin, something in the clumsy deliberation of the tedious movements unspeakably nasty. Even at this first encounter, this first glimpse, I was overcome with disgust and dread.

From *The War of the Worlds* by H.G. Wells.

Activities

Alternative point of view

In the passage, a narrator is telling the story from a **first person viewpoint** – 'I saw a young man … I narrowly missed being …' Everything that happens is described through his eyes. Many other witnesses were present, however.

I You are going to write a description of this same strange event through another person's eyes – that of the young male shop assistant who was actually standing on the cylinder.

   a List the sequence of events from the young man's point of view.

   b Think about the effect the events would have on the young man.

   c Describe the scene (and the young man's feelings) from a *first person viewpoint* – write as though you are the young man, using 'I …'

Radio script

On Hallowe'en night in 1938, a famous radio play produced by Orson Welles was broadcast in America. Welles cleverly changed the setting of *The War of the Worlds* story from London in the 1890s to contemporary America. The story was told through a series of realistic-sounding radio news bulletins.

It began with a studio announcement:

'We interrupt this programme to bring you a live, outside broadcast from Grovers Mill, New Jersey, where a strange cylinder has just landed.'

Then, an actor playing the radio reporter said,

'A cylinder is unscrewing and a large, unearthly creature is wriggling out and...'

It wasn't long before thousands of people in all parts of the country started to panic. There were frantic telephone calls to radio stations and to the police. The streets were suddenly full of terrified people. One man was reported to have come home to find his wife clutching a bottle of poison. She was screaming, 'I would rather die *this* way than *that!*'

When the hoax was revealed the next day, the name of Orson Welles became world-famous.

You are going to write the opening to a radio script similar to that of Orson Welles.

1 You will need to think about the following if you are to convince a modern audience that a Martian invasion is actually taking place:
   • what is to be said?
   • who is to say it?
   • will you use interviews, journalists' reports, or both?
2 Set it in contemporary Britain and make the invasion sound realistic for a British audience.

A last embrace

This highly dramatic scene takes place as Catherine is dying in childbirth. Her husband, Edgar Linton, is on his way back from church. This is Cathy's final farewell from Heathcliff, her true love. Nelly, the servant, is witnessing the scene.

'Do come to me, Heathcliff.'

In her eagerness she rose, and supported herself on the arm of the chair. At that earnest appeal, he turned to her, looking absolutely desperate. His eyes wide, and wet, at last, flashed fiercely on her; his breast heaved convulsively. An instant they held **asunder**; and then how they met I hardly saw, but Catherine made a spring, and he caught her, and they were locked in an embrace from which I thought my mistress would never be released alive. In fact, to my eyes, she seemed directly insensible. He flung himself into the nearest seat, and on my approaching hurriedly to ascertain if she had fainted, he gnashed at me, and foamed like a mad dog, and gathered her to him with greedy jealousy. I did not feel as if I were in the company of a creature of my own species; it appeared that he would not understand, though I spoke to him; so, I stood off, and held my tongue, in great perplexity.

A movement of Catherine's relieved me a little presently: she put up her hand to clasp his neck, and bring her cheek to his, as he held her: while he, in return, covering her with frantic caresses, said wildly –

'You teach me now how cruel you've been – cruel and false. *Why* did you despise me? *Why* did you betray your own heart, Cathy? I have not one word of comfort – you deserve this. You have killed yourself. Yes, you may kiss me, and cry; and wring out my kisses and tears. They'll blight you – they'll damn you. You loved me – then what *right* had you

asunder – apart

to leave me? What right – answer me – for the poor fancy you felt for Linton? Because misery, and degradation, and death, and nothing that God or Satan could inflict would have parted us, *you*, of your own will, did it. I have not broken your heart – *you* have broken it – and in breaking it, you have broken mine. So much the worse for me, that I am strong. Do I want to live? What kind of living will it be when you – oh, God! would *you* like to live with your soul in the grave?'

'Let me alone. Let me alone,' sobbed Catherine. 'If I've done wrong, I'm dying for it. It is enough! You left me too; but I won't upbraid you! I forgive you. Forgive me!'

'It is hard to forgive, and to look at those eyes, and feel those wasted hands,' he answered. 'Kiss me again; and don't let me see your eyes! I forgive what you have done to me. I love *my* murderer – but *yours*! How can I?'

They were silent – their faces hid against each other, and washed by each other's tears. At least, I suppose the weeping was on both sides; as it seemed Heathcliff *could* weep on a great occasion like this.

I grew very uncomfortable, meanwhile; for the afternoon wore fast away, the man whom I had sent off returned from his errand, and I could distinguish, by the shine of the westering sun up the valley, a **concourse** thickening outside Gimmerton chapel porch.

'Service is over,' I announced. 'My master will be here in half an hour.'

Heathcliff groaned a curse, and strained Catherine closer – she never moved.

Ere long I perceived a group of the servants passing up the road towards the kitchen wing. Mr Linton was not far behind; he opened the gate himself, and sauntered slowly up, probably enjoying the lovely afternoon that breathed as soft as summer.

---

concourse – crowd

'Now he is here,' I exclaimed. 'For Heaven's sake, hurry down! You'll not meet any one on the front stairs. Do be quick; and stay among the trees till he is fairly in.'

'I must go, Cathy,' said Heathcliff, seeking to extricate himself from his companion's arms. 'But, if I live, I'll see you again before you are asleep. I won't stay five yards from your window.'

'You must not go!' she answered, holding him as firmly as her strength allowed. 'You shall not, I tell you.'

'For one hour,' he pleaded earnestly.

'Not for one minute,' she replied.

'I *must* – Linton will be up immediately,' persisted the alarmed intruder.

He would have risen, and unfixed her fingers by the act – she clung fast, gasping; there was mad resolution in her face.

'No!' she shrieked. 'Oh, don't, don't go. It is the last time! Edgar will not hurt us. Heathcliff, I shall die! I shall die!'

'Damn the fool! There he is,' cried Heathcliff, sinking back into his seat. 'Hush, my darling! Hush, hush, Catherine! I'll stay. If he shot me so, I'd expire with a blessing on my lips.'

And there they were fast again. I heard my master mounting the stairs – the cold sweat ran from my forehead; I was horrified.

From *Wuthering Heights*
by Emily Brontë

Activities

Heathcliff's reactions

I Read the description of Heathcliff carefully. Pick out the key words and phrases that describe him in this passage, for example, 'absolutely desperate', 'eyes wide and wet'.

2 At this emotional time, Heathcliff's speech is full of questions and exclamations. He is both loving and harsh. With a partner, take it in turns to speak Heathcliff's words aloud. As your partner is reading, make a note of:

a some of the descriptive words Heathcliff uses

b the types of phrases Heathcliff uses (e.g. are they long or short? are they repetitive?).

Predictions

I What will happen next? Continue the story for three or four more paragraphs, using description and speech. You should:
- describe Edgar Linton's reaction to the scene
- include Nelly's reactions
- show what is happening to Cathy
- try to make Heathcliff's words to Edgar Linton sound as authentic as possible.

2 You might like to compare your version with *Wuthering Heights*, chapter 16.

Ways of telling

LOADING THE RAFT

SILAS MAKES A DISCOVERY

THE CREATURE COMES TO LIFE

Loading the raft

When Robinson Crusoe is shipwrecked he is the only survivor. He manages to swim ashore to a desert island, where he makes a raft. He then returns to the ship to take anything which may be useful to him until he is rescued.

My raft was now strong enough to bear any reasonable weight. My next care was what to load it with, and how to preserve what I laid upon it from the surf of the sea; but I was not long considering this. I first laid all the planks or boards upon it that I could get, and having considered well what I most wanted, I first got three of the seamen's chests, which I had broken open and emptied, and lowered them down upon my raft. The first of these I filled with provisions, viz., bread, rice, three Dutch cheeses, five pieces of dried goat's flesh, which we lived much upon, and a little remainder of European corn, which had been laid by for some

fowls which we brought to sea with us, but the fowls were killed. There had been some barley and wheat together, but, to my great disappointment, I found afterwards that the rats had eaten or spoiled it all. As for liquors, I found several cases of bottles belonging to our skipper, in which were some cordial waters, and, in all, about five or six gallons of **rack.** These I stowed by themselves, there being no need to put them into the chest, nor no room for them. While I was doing this, I found the tide began to flow, though very calm, and I had the mortification to see my coat, shirt, and waistcoat, which I had left on shore upon the sand, swim away; as for my breeches, which were only linen, and open-kneed, I swam on board in them, and my stockings. However, this put me upon rummaging for clothes, of which I found enough, but took no more than I wanted for present use; for I had other things which my eye was more upon, as first tools to work with on shore; and it was after long searching that I found out the carpenter's chest, which was indeed a very useful prize to me, and much more valuable than a ship-loading of gold would have been at that time. I got it down to my raft, even whole as it was, without losing time to look into it, for I knew in general what it contained.

My next care was for some ammunition and arms; there were two very good fowling-pieces in the great cabin, and two pistols; these I secured first, with some powder-horns, and a small bag of shot, and two old rusty swords. I knew there were three barrels of powder in the ship, but knew not where our gunner had stowed them; but with much search I found them, two of them dry and good, the third had taken water; those two I got to my raft with the arms. And now I thought myself pretty well freighted, and began to think how I should get to shore with them, having neither sail, oar, or rudder; and the least capful of wind would have overset all my navigation.

From *Robinson Crusoe* by Daniel Defoe

rack – alcoholic drink

Activities

Investigating the text

1 Read the passage carefully to find out what Robinson Crusoe took off the ship.

2 Draw up a chart like the one below.

a In the left-hand column, list the things which Robinson Crusoe loaded on his raft from the ship.

b In the right-hand column note down how these might be useful to him.

What he takes off the ship	How this may be useful to him
Three seamen's chests.	Storage.
Bread, rice, cheese.	Food to eat until he can grow his own.
Corn.	

Following on

3 Six months later Robinson Crusoe is beginning to establish himself on his island. Write an extract from his diary where he explains how he has survived. Remember that he will comment and reflect on all sorts of things including:

- how he has used the things he brought from the ship
- what would have been useful to him
- the things he is missing (such as people, or some sorts of food, perhaps)
- the adventures he has had.

Silas makes a discovery

Some time ago Silas Marner, who lived only to make money, had his savings stolen from him. He was deeply affected by the loss. Silas became a miserly, inward-looking man, obsessed with money and memories of his gold. However, something happens which is to change everything …

Turning towards the hearth, where the two logs had fallen apart, and sent forth only a red uncertain glimmer, he seated himself on his fireside chair, and was stooping to push his logs together, when, to his blurred vision, it seemed as if there were gold on the floor in front of the hearth. Gold! – his own gold – brought back to him as mysteriously as it had been taken away! He felt his heart begin to beat violently, and for a few moments he was unable to stretch out his hand and grasp the restored treasure. The heap of gold seemed to glow and get larger beneath his agitated gaze. He leaned forward at last, and stretched forth his hand; but instead of the hard coin with the familiar resisting outline, his fingers encountered soft warm curls. In utter amazement, Silas fell on his knees and bent his head low to examine the marvel: it was a sleeping child – a round, fair thing, with soft yellow rings all over its head. Could this be his little sister come back to him in a dream – his little sister who he had carried about in his arms for a year before she died, when he was a small boy without shoes or stockings?
That was the first thought that darted across Silas' blank wonderment. *Was* it a dream? He rose to his feet again, pushed his logs together, and, throwing on some dried leaves and sticks, raised a flame; but the flame did not disperse the vision – it only lit up more distinctly the little round form of the child and its shabby clothing.
It was very much like his little sister. Silas sank into his chair powerless.

✳ ✳ ✳

But there was a cry on the hearth: the child had awaked, and Marner stooped to lift it on his knee. It clung round his neck, and burst louder and louder into that mingling of inarticulate cries with 'mammy' by which little children express the bewilderment of waking. Silas pressed it to him, and almost unconsciously uttered sounds of hushing tenderness, while he bethought himself that some of his porridge, which had got cool by the dying fire, would do to feed the child with if it were only warmed up a little.

He had plenty to do through the next hour. The porridge, sweetened with some dry brown sugar from an old store which he had refrained from using for himself, stopped the cries of the little one, and made her lift her blue eyes with a wide quiet gaze at Silas, as he put the spoon into her mouth. Presently she slipped from his knee and began to toddle about, but with a pretty stagger that made Silas jump up and follow her lest she should fall against anything that would hurt her. But she only fell in a sitting posture on the ground, and began to pull at her boots, looking up at him with a crying face as if the boots hurt her. He took her on his knee again, but it was some time before it occurred to Silas' dull bachelor mind that the wet boots were the grievance, pressing on her warm ankles. He got them off with difficulty, and baby was at once happily occupied with the primary mystery of her own toes.

From *Silas Marner* by George Eliot

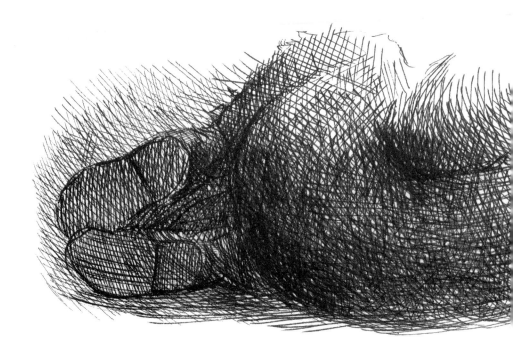

Activities

Associations

1 What does gold mean to you? Write the word in the centre of a blank sheet of paper and then draw out in a 'spider-plan' all the associations or connections that you can make with the idea of 'gold'. Work in pairs and try to make as many connections as you can.

Treasure — GOLD — Golden glow
— Coins

New qualities

2 Silas was an obsessive character, locked into memories of the gold he had lost. But now, with the discovery of the child – his new-found treasure – his personality changes dramatically. The gold and the child are clearly linked in the passage. Take each of the qualities associated with gold from your spider-plan. Write briefly about the ways each of these are linked to Silas after he has found the child. For example:

> There is a 'golden glow' in Silas' cottage from the child's golden hair.
> Silas feels a 'golden glow' of warmth towards the child.

Symbols

One dictionary definition of a symbol is 'something which is used to suggest or represent something else – for example, a dove is a symbol of peace.'

You have already thought and written about some of the symbolic links between a young child and gold. Now you are going to think about the kind of person you could associate with such things as *ice*, *fire*, *steel*, or *plastic* – for example 'a man of steel', 'the ice maiden'.

1 Choose ice, fire, steel, plastic, or another material.

2 List some of the associations with the word you have chosen (perhaps in the form of a spider-plan).

3 Write a short description of a person who could be linked symbolically with the word you have chosen. Include your original ideas and associations.

The creature comes to life

Dr Frankenstein has been working on 'a new discovery' for two long years. He is now ready to put his discovery to the test.

It was on a dreary night of November, that I beheld the accomplishment of my toils. With an anxiety that almost amounted to agony, I collected the instruments of life around me, that I might **infuse** a spark of being into the lifeless thing that lay at my feet. It was already one in the morning; the rain pattered dismally against the panes, and my candle was nearly burnt out, when, by the glimmer of the half-extinguished light, I saw the dull yellow eye of the creature open; it breathed hard, and a **convulsive** motion agitated its limbs.

How can I describe my emotions at this catastrophe, or how **delineate** the wretch whom with such infinite pains and care I had endeavoured to form? His limbs were in proportion, and I had selected his features as beautiful. Beautiful! – Great God! His yellow skin scarcely covered the work of muscles and arteries beneath; his hair was of a **lustrous** black, and flowing; his teeth of pearly whiteness; but these **luxuriances** only formed a more horrid contrast with his watery eyes, that seemed almost of the same colour as the dun-white sockets in which they were set, his shrivelled complexion and straight black lips. The different accidents of life are not so changeable as the feelings of human nature. I had worked hard for nearly two years, for the sole purpose of infusing life into an **inanimate** body. For this I had deprived myself of rest and

---

infuse – pour   **convulsive** – violently jerky   **delineate** – describe
lustrous – glossy, shining   **luxuriances** – (here) handsome features
inanimate – lifeless

health. I had desired it with an **ardour** that far exceeded moderation; but now that I had finished, the beauty of the dream vanished, and breathless horror and disgust filled my heart. Unable to endure the aspect of the being I had created, I rushed out of the room, and continued a long time **traversing** my bedchamber, unable to compose my mind to sleep. At length **lassitude** succeeded to the **tumult** I had before endured; and I threw myself on the bed in my clothes, endeavouring to seek a few moments of forgetfulness. But it was in vain: I slept, indeed, but I was disturbed by the wildest dreams. I thought I saw Elizabeth, in the bloom of health, walking in the streets of Ingolstadt. Delighted and surprised, I embraced her, but as I imprinted the first kiss on her lips, they became livid with the **hue** of death; her features appeared to change, and I thought that I held the corpse of my dead mother in my arms; a **shroud** enveloped her form, and I saw the grave-worms crawling in the folds of flannel. I started from my sleep with horror; a cold dew covered my forehead, my teeth chattered, and every limb became convulsed: when, by the dim and yellow light of the moon, as it forced its way through the window shutters, I beheld the wretch – the miserable monster whom I had created. He held up the curtain of the bed; and his eyes, if eyes they may be called, were fixed on me. His jaws opened, and he muttered some inarticulate sounds, while a grin wrinkled his cheeks. He might have spoken, but I did not hear; one hand was stretched out, seemingly to detain me, but I escaped, and rushed downstairs. I took refuge in the courtyard belonging to the house which I inhabited; where I remained during the rest of the night, walking up and down in the greatest agitation, listening attentively, catching and fearing each sound as if it were to announce the approach of the **demoniacal** corpse to which I had so miserably given life.

From *Frankenstein* by Mary Shelley

---

ardour – intense passion   **traversing** – walking up and down
lassitude – tiredness   **tumult** – emotional upset   **hue** – colour
shroud – cloth in which a dead body is wrapped   **demoniacal** – like a demon

Activities

The extract tells the famous scene from the novel *Frankenstein* where the scientist, Dr Victor Frankenstein, brings his creature to life. You may well have seen this moment depicted in a number of film versions. In each description, a range of familiar ingredients are usually brought together:

- a crashing thunderstorm with violent streaks of lightning
- an old castle with high ceilings, swinging lanterns and shadows flickering across walls
- a wild, eccentric scientist totally absorbed in his work
- the shocking appearance of the monster itself as it slowly comes to life.

Look at the questions on the next page. They help you think about how these stereotypical ingredients might compare with the original text.

Novel v. film

Look closely at the passage and see *how* it differs from the scene as shown in the various film versions.

I How does the passage describe each of the following?
- the **setting**, where the experiment is taking place
- the **description of the creature** as it gradually comes to life
- the **personality of Dr Frankenstein** – his thoughts, feelings and fears about his creation.

Write down as much as you can about these three areas, using Mary Shelley's words.

2 How do these descriptions fit in with the range of 'familiar ingredients' described on page 73?

Interview

You are going to write an imaginary magazine interview with Dr Frankenstein.

I Think about:
- why Dr Frankenstein wanted to create the creature
- how he hoped his creature might turn out
- how his feelings changed as the creature came to life.

2 Improvise the interview with a partner, to help you with ideas for your writing. You will have to guess some of the answers, but you will be able to base others on what you have read in the extract.

3 Write down your questions (keep them short) and Dr Frankenstein's answers as you might read them in a magazine.

Creating atmosphere

'Quiet. Very quiet'

Scrooge is being shown by the Ghost of Christmas Future how great sorrow has fallen on the Cratchit family after the death of the young boy, Tiny Tim. Everyone is trying to be brave.

The Ghost conducted him through several streets familiar to his feet; and as they went along, Scrooge looked here and there to find himself, but nowhere was he to be seen. They entered poor Bob Cratchit's house; the dwelling he had visited before; and found the mother and the children seated round the fire.

Quiet. Very quiet. The noisy little Cratchits were as still as statues in one corner, and sat looking up at Peter, who had a book before him. The mother and her daughters were engaged in sewing. But surely they were very quiet!

' "And He took a child, and set him in the midst of them." '

Where had Scrooge heard those words? He had not dreamed them. The boy must have read them out, as he and the Spirit crossed the threshold. Why did he not go on?

The mother laid her work upon the table, and put her hand up to her face.

'The colour hurts my eyes,' she said.

The colour? Ah, poor Tiny Tim!

'They're better now again,' said Cratchit's wife. 'It makes them weak by candle-light; and I wouldn't show weak eyes to your father when he comes home, for the world. It must be near his time.'

'Past it rather,' Peter answered, shutting up his book. 'But I think he's walked a little slower than he used, these few last evenings, mother.'

They were very quiet again. At last she said, and in a steady, cheerful voice, that only faltered once:

'I have known him walk with – I have known him walk with Tiny Tim upon his shoulder, very fast indeed.'

'And so have I,' cried Peter. 'Often.'

'And so have I!' exclaimed another. So had all.

'But he was very light to carry,' she resumed, intent upon her work, 'and his father loved him so, that it was no trouble – no trouble. And there is your father at the door!'

She hurried out to meet him; and little Bob in his **comforter** – he had needed of it, poor fellow – came in. His tea was ready for him on the hob, and they all tried who should help him to it most. Then the two young Cratchits got upon his knees and laid, each child a little cheek, against his face, as if they said, 'Don't mind it, father. Don't be grieved!'

From *A Christmas Carol* by Charles Dickens

comforter – long woollen scarf

Activities

Can you find

1 The part where someone tries to hide her tears?

2 A quotation from the Bible that the family members are using to comfort themselves?

3 A part where the family show they are worried about Bob Cratchit's reaction to his son's death?

Creating atmosphere

The atmosphere Dickens has created is one of quietness and sorrow. The family is waiting for Bob Cratchit's return from work. They are trying to be brave, but their sadness shows through. They want to comfort one another, but words are not enough.

1 You are going to act out a similar situation in groups of three or four. You will be sitting in a room waiting for some news. Everyone will be very tense, but you will all be trying to support one another and not panic.

   a In your groups, decide whether you will be a family, or a group of friends or neighbours

   b Decide what news you are waiting to hear. (It should be something very important.)

   c Agree three main points about each character's personality and decide who will play each character.

   d Each of you should think about why the news is so important to your character, and then you should discuss your ideas with the rest of the group.

   e Act out the situation. Remember, this is taking place before the news arrives.

2 Write a short scene, using the ideas that have come from acting the situation above. Use the following to bring out the tension of the atmosphere:
- dialogue
- description
- direct statements
- implication or indirect statements.

Your careful reading of Dickens' writing should help you in this task.

A reckless ride

Tess Durbeyfield, a young country girl, has accepted a lift in a horse-drawn gig. The driver, reckless Alec d'Urberville, is making the horse go at a full gallop.

Down, down, they sped, the wheels humming like a top, the dogcart rocking right and left, its axis acquiring a slightly oblique set in relation to the line of progress; the figure of the horse rising and falling in undulations before them. Sometimes a wheel was off the ground, it seemed, for many yards; sometimes a stone was sent spinning over the hedge, and flinty sparks from the horse's hoofs outshone the daylight. The aspect of the straight road enlarged with their advance, the two banks dividing like a splitting stick; one rushing past at each shoulder.

The wind blew through Tess's white muslin to her very skin, and her washed hair flew out behind. She was determined to show no open fear, but she clutched d'Urberville's rein-arm.

'Don't touch my arm! We shall be thrown out if you do! Hold on round my waist!'

She grasped his waist, and so they reached the bottom. 'Safe, thank God, in spite of your fooling!' said she, her face on fire.

'Tess – fie! that's temper!' said d'Urberville.

''Tis truth.'

'Well, you need not let go your hold of me so thanklessly the moment you feel yourself out of danger.'

She had not considered what she had been doing; whether he were man or woman, stick or stone, in her involuntary hold on him. Recovering her reserve she sat without replying, and thus they reached the summit of another **declivity**.

'Now then, again!' said d'Urberville.

'No, no!' said Tess. 'Show more sense, do, please.'

⫸

---

declivity – slope

'But when people find themselves on one of the highest points in the county, they must get down again,' he retorted.

He loosed rein, and away they went a second time. D'Urberville turned his face to her as they rocked, and said, in playful **raillery**: 'Now then, put your arms round my waist again, as you did before, my Beauty.'

'Never!' said Tess independently, holding on as well as she could without touching him.

'Let me put one little kiss on those holmberry lips, Tess, or even on that warmed cheek, and I'll stop – on my honour I will!'

Tess, surprised beyond measure, slid farther back still on her seat, at which he urged the horse anew, and rocked her the more.

'Will nothing else do?' she cried at length, in desperation, her large eyes staring at him like those of a wild animal. This dressing her up so prettily by her mother had apparently been to lamentable purpose.

'Nothing, dear Tess,' he replied.

'Oh, I don't know – very well; I don't mind!' she panted miserably.

He drew rein, and as they slowed he was on the point of imprinting the desired salute, when, as if hardly yet aware of her own modesty, she dodged aside. His arms being occupied with the reins there was left him no power to prevent her manoeuvre.

'Now, damn it – I'll break both our necks!' swore her **capriciously** passionate companion.

From *Tess of the d'Urbervilles* by Thomas Hardy

---

raillery – jokiness, banter **capriciously** – full of whims, constantly changing

Activities

Close reading

Look carefully at the first paragraph.

1 Write out three phrases which give you an impression of **speed**. After each phrase, write a sentence explaining how it gives you this feeling.

2 Write out three phrases which give you an impression of **danger**. After each phrase, write a sentence explaining how it gives you this feeling.

3 Hardy says that Tess 'was determined to show no open fear', but there are clues to indicate that she is frightened. What are they?

4 How does Mr d'Urberville try to take advantage of Tess?

5 How does Tess outwit Mr d'Urberville?

A reckless ride

1 Write your own story of 'a reckless ride'. In the story the main character will try to trap a member of the opposite sex by using speed and danger to create fear.
   • Choose a setting where speed plays an important part, for example a fairground ride, or a lift home by motor bike or fast car.
   • Think of a character who is reckless and rather wild, who will not take 'no' for an answer.

2 Follow the pattern of the passage above so that your story includes:
   • a description of the speed and danger
   • conversation between the two people
   • another burst of speed
   • further conversation
   • ending.

Attack by Heat-Ray

Martian invaders have emerged from their cylinders, to construct terrifying killing machines armed with deadly Heat-Rays. The following attack takes place near the River Thames.

At that I ducked at once under water, and, holding my breath until movement was an agony, blundered painfully ahead under the surface as long as I could. The water was in a tumult about me, and rapidly growing hotter.

When for a moment I raised my head to take breath and throw the hair and water from my eyes, the steam was rising in a whirling white fog that at first hid the Martians altogether. The noise was deafening. Then I saw them dimly, colossal figures of grey, magnified by the mist. They had passed by me, and two were stooping over the frothing, tumultuous ruins of their comrade.

The third and fourth stood beside him in the water, one perhaps two hundred yards from me, the other towards Laleham. The generators of the Heat-Rays waved high, and the hissing beams smote down this way and that.

The air was full of sound, a deafening and confusing conflict of noises – the **clangorous din** of the Martians, the crash of falling houses, the thud of trees, fences, sheds flashing into flame, and the crackling and roaring of fire. Dense black smoke was leaping up to mingle with the steam from the river, and as the Heat-Ray went to and fro over Weybridge its impact was marked by flashes of **incandescent** white, that gave place at once to a smoky dance of **lurid** flames. The nearer houses still stood intact, awaiting their fate, shadowy, faint, and **pallid** in the steam, with the fire behind them going to and fro.

For a moment perhaps I stood there, breast-high in the almost boiling water, dumbfounded at my position, hopeless of escape. Through the **reek** I could see the people who had been with me in the river

clangorous din – loud metallic noise   **incandescent** – white-hot, glowing
lurid – vivid, glaring   **pallid** – pale   **reek** – smoke

scrambling out of the water through the reeds, like little frogs hurrying through grass from the advance of a man, or running to and fro in utter dismay on the towing-path.

Then suddenly the white flashes of the Heat-Ray came leaping towards me. The houses caved in as they dissolved at its touch, and darted out flames; the trees changed to fire with a roar. The Ray flickered up and down the towing-path, licking off the people who ran this way and that, and came down to the water's edge not fifty yards from where I stood. It swept across the river to Shepperton, and the water in its track rose in a boiling **weal** crested with steam. I turned shoreward.

In another moment the huge wave, well-nigh at the boiling-point, had rushed upon me. I screamed aloud, and scalded, half-blinded, agonised, I staggered through the leaping, hissing water towards the shore. Had my foot stumbled, it would have been the end. I fell helplessly, in full sight of the Martians, upon the broad, bare gravelly spit that runs down to mark the angle of the Wey and Thames. I expected nothing but death.

I have a dim memory of the foot of a Martian coming down within a score of yards of my head, driving straight into the loose gravel, whirling it this way and that, and lifting again; of a long suspense, and then of the four carrying the **débris** of their comrade between them, now clear and then presently faint through a veil of smoke, receding interminably, as it seemed to me, across a vast space of river and meadow. And then, very slowly, I realised that by a miracle I had escaped.

From *The War of the Worlds* by H.G. Wells

weal – ridge   **débris** – wreckage

Activities

Making it clear

There is a lot going on in this passage, but are you clear about what is actually happening? It is easier to work this out if you start by identifying the important stages in the description. For example:

Stage 1: the narrator ducks under water and holds his breath for as long as possible.

Stage 2: the narrator raises his head and sees the Martians.

1 Continue to identify the main stages in the description.

2 Briefly describe each stage, using your own words.

Building suspense

The key stages you have just described build up and then hold an atmosphere of suspense throughout the passage. Write your own short piece in which you try to build suspense.

1 Begin by focusing on a single moment, rather than thinking about a complete story. Possible starting points might include:
   - You are walking home at night when you start to hear footsteps approaching from behind …
   - You are the last person left in school; you are about to switch off the light and walk down the corridor when …
   - You have wandered into your eccentric uncle's cellar when the batteries in your torch begin to fade…

2 Then build up the suspense step by step.

3 Your story should end with something – a person or event – which *suddenly* changes what has been happening as you built up the suspense.

Over to you …

Catching sight of the monster

Dr Frankenstein has received some tragic family news. He decides to travel to his home town of Geneva.

It was completely dark when I arrived in the environs of Geneva; the gates of the town were already shut; and I was obliged to pass the night at Secheron, a village at the distance of half a league from the city. The sky was serene; and as I was unable to rest, I resolved to visit the spot where my poor William had been murdered. As I could not pass through the town, I was obliged to cross the lake in a boat to arrive at Plainpalais. During this short voyage I saw the lightnings playing on the summit of Mont Blanc in the most beautiful figures. The storm appeared to approach rapidly; and, on landing, I ascended a low hill, that I might observe its progress. It advanced; the heavens were clouded, and I soon felt the rain coming slowly in large drops, but its violence quickly increased.

❋　❋　❋

While I watched the tempest, so beautiful yet terrific, I wandered on with a hasty step. This noble war in the sky elevated my spirits; I clasped my hands and exclaimed aloud, 'William, dear angel! this is thy funeral, this thy **dirge!**' As I said these words, I perceived in the gloom a figure which stole from behind a clump of trees near me; I stood fixed, gazing intently: I could not be mistaken. A flash of lightning illuminated the object, and discovered its shape plainly to me; its gigantic stature, and the deformity of its aspect, more hideous than belongs to humanity, instantly informed me that it was the wretch, the filthy daemon to whom I had given life. What did he there? Could he be (I shuddered at the conception) the murderer of my brother? No sooner did that idea cross my imagination, than I became convinced of its truth; my teeth chattered, and I was forced to lean against a tree for support. The figure passed me quickly, and I lost it in the gloom. Nothing in human shape could have destroyed that fair child. *He* was

dirge – funeral song

thc murderer! I could not doubt it. The mere presence of the idea was an irresistible proof of the fact. I thought of pursuing the devil; but it would have been in vain, for another flash discovered him to me hanging among the rocks of the nearly perpendicular ascent of Mount Salêve, a hill that bound Plainpalais on the south. He soon reached the summit, and disappeared.

I remained motionless. The thunder ceased, but the rain still continued, and the scene was enveloped in an impenetrable darkness. I revolved in my mind the events which I had until now sought to forget: the whole train of my progress towards the creation; the appearance of the work of my own hands alive at my bedside; its departure. Two years had now nearly elapsed since the night on which he first received life; and was this his first crime? Alas! I had turned loose into the world a **depraved** wretch, whose delight was in **carnage** and misery; had he not murdered my brother?

From *Frankenstein* by Mary Shelley

depraved – evil, corrupt   **carnage** – bloodshed, slaughter

Activities

Who was William?

1 This passage is narrated by Dr Frankenstein. As readers we soon learn that William has been murdered. What exactly are we told about William? Read through the passage once again and then note down everything you can learn about William.

2 Compare your notes with a partner's.

A film treatment

3 This scene is described in a vivid and exciting way. Imagine that you have been asked to present it as a film version. Using the film storyboard format on the next page, work out your ideas for a film 'treatment'. You will need to give directions for:
- lighting
- camera angles
- types of shot (close-ups, mid-shots, long-shots etc)
- sound effects
- music
- voice-over
- dialogue.

Shot				Action
1				The scene opens at night with
	Close			Dr Frankenstein arriving at a
	Medium			small Swiss village – in the
				distance it is just possible to
	Long	↘	SOUND: Music – moody and slow	glimpse the lights of a large city –
				Geneva.

Shot				Action
2				Close-up of Dr Frankenstein in a
	Close	↘		doorway. He asks for a room for
	Medium			the night and goes into the house.
	Long		SOUND: Dr F: Have you a room free tonight? Innkeeper: Yes, come this way …	

Shot				Action
	Close			
	Medium			
	Long		SOUND:	

Reporting

THE MAID AND THE MURDERER

OUTLINING THE CASE

REPORTS OF THE MARTIAN INVASION

AN OFFICIAL REPORT ON THE CONTENTS OF GULLIVER'S POCKETS

The maid and the murderer

Throughout the story of *The Strange Case of Dr Jekyll and Mr Hyde* we hear about a mysterious Mr Hyde who makes people feel very frightened. In the following extract we read of a terrible crime he has committed.

Nearly a year later, in the month of October, 18—, London was startled by a crime … The details were few and startling. A maid-servant living alone in a house not far from the river had gone upstairs to bed about eleven. Although a fog rolled over the city in the **small hours**, the early part of the night was cloudless, and the lane, which the maid's window overlooked, was brilliantly lit by the full moon. It seems she was romantically given; for she sat down upon her box, which stood immediately under the window, and fell into a dream of musing. Never … had she felt more at peace with all men or thought more kindly of the world. And as she so sat she became aware of an aged and beautiful gentleman with white hair drawing near along the lane; and advancing to meet him, another and very small gentleman, to whom at first she paid less attention. When they had come within speech (which was just under the maid's eyes) the older man bowed and **accosted** the other

small hours – just after midnight   **accosted** – approached in order to speak to

with a very pretty manner of politeness. It did not seem as if the subject of his address were of great importance; indeed, from his pointing, it sometimes appeared as if he were only inquiring his way; but the moon shone on his face as he spoke, and the girl was pleased to watch it, it seemed to breathe such an innocent and old-world kindness of **disposition**, yet with something high too, as of a well-founded self-content. Presently her eye wandered to the other, and she was surprised to recognise in him a certain Mr Hyde, who had once visited her master and for whom she had conceived a dislike. He had in his hand a heavy cane, with which he was **trifling**; but he answered never a word, and seemed to listen with an ill-contained impatience. And then all of a sudden he broke out in a great flame of anger, stamping with his foot, brandishing the cane, and carrying on (as the maid described it) like a madman. The old gentleman took a step back, with the air of one very much surprised and a trifle hurt; and at that Mr Hyde broke out of all bounds, and clubbed him to the earth. And next moment, with ape-like fury, he was trampling his victim under foot, and hailing down a storm of blows, under which the bones were audibly shattered and the body jumped upon the roadway. At the horror of these sights and sounds, the maid fainted.

It was two o'clock when she came to herself and called for the police. The murderer was gone long ago; but there lay his victim in the middle of the lane, incredibly mangled. The stick with which the deed had been done, although it was of some rare and very tough and heavy wood, had broken in the middle under the stress of this **insensate** cruelty; and one splintered half had rolled in the neighbouring gutter – the other, without doubt, had been carried away by the murderer. A purse and a gold watch were found upon the victim; but, no cards or papers, except a sealed and stamped envelope, which he had been probably carrying to the post, and which bore the name and address of Mr Utterson.

From *The Strange Case of Dr Jekyll and Mr Hyde* by Robert Louis Stevenson

disposition – nature, character **trifling** – fidgeting **insensate** – unfeeling

Activities

Police interview with key witness

All of London has been shocked by the brutal murder of Sir Danvers Carew. There is one key witness who saw what happened and can identify the possible murderer.

1 Work in pairs. One of you will be a police officer sent to investigate the crime, the other will be the maid who witnessed what happened.

2 Carefully reread the passage so that you can collect the information you need for your interview.

a **Police officer** – make a list of questions that you want to ask the witness. You will need to establish from her all sorts of details, such as:
  • the time it happened
  • the weather
  • where the maid was sitting
  • what she saw
  • description of the attacker.

b **Maid** – make sure you have the story straight, with a clear outline of what you saw.

3 Now act out the actual interview. If possible, tape record your interview.

Outlining the case

Sherlock Holmes, the famous detective, listens to the story told to him by Helen Stoner, the distraught young woman we have met in an earlier extract. She tells him how she witnessed the death of her sister in very mysterious circumstances.

I could not sleep that night. A vague feeling of impending misfortune impressed me. My sister and I, you will recollect, were twins, and you know how subtle are the links which bind two souls which are so closely allied. It was a wild night. The wind was howling outside, and the rain was beating and splashing against the windows. Suddenly, amid all the hubbub of the gale, there burst forth the wild scream of a terrified woman. I knew that it was my sister's voice. I sprang from my bed, wrapped a shawl round me, and rushed into the corridor. As I opened my door I seemed to hear a low whistle, such as my sister described, and a few moments later a clanging sound, as if a mass of metal had fallen. As I ran down the passage, my sister's door was unlocked, and revolved slowly upon its hinges. I stared at it horror-stricken, not knowing what was about to issue from it. By the light of the corridor-lamp I saw my sister appear at the opening, her face **blanched** with terror, her hands groping for help, her whole figure swaying to and fro like that of a drunkard. I ran to her and threw my arms round her, but at that moment her knees seemed to give way and she fell to the ground. She writhed as one who is in terrible pain, and her limbs were dreadfully convulsed. At first I thought that she had not recognised me, but as I bent over her she suddenly shrieked out in a voice which I shall never forget, 'Oh, my God! Helen! It was the band! The speckled band!' There was something else which she **would fain** have said, and she stabbed with her finger into the air in the direction of the doctor's room, but a fresh convulsion seized her and choked her words. I rushed out, calling loudly for my

blanched – turned white **would fain** – would have liked to

stepfather, and I met him hastening from his room in his dressing-gown. When he reached my sister's side she was unconscious, and though he poured brandy down her throat and sent for medical aid from the village, all efforts were in vain, for she slowly sank and died without having recovered her consciousness. Such was the dreadful end of my beloved sister.

From *The Adventure of the Speckled Band* by Arthur Conan Doyle

Activities

Checking the facts

Imagine you are a detective like Sherlock Holmes.

1 Look back carefully through Helen Stoner's account and spot the important facts about the events that night. You should be able to find at least ten facts.

2 Record your observations in your notebook, as an investigator would.

3 Make a table like the one below. In the first column, note your facts. In the second column, note down the significance of the facts you have discovered.

What happened that night	Why this might be important
Feeling of impending misfortune.	She felt as though her twin sister was in trouble.
Stormy night.	Sounds of storm would cover other noises. Help could not reach the house easily.
Screams of terrified woman.	
Low whistle.	

Continue the detective story

Helen Stoner has come to see Sherlock Holmes because she fears for her life. She is afraid that the terrible events of the night when her sister died may be repeated, but that this time she will be the victim. She wants Sherlock Holmes to solve the mystery of her sister's death before she, too, is killed.

1 Using the information you have gathered in your investigator's notebook as a basis, take up the threads of the story and continue it. Your story could be told by:
   • the young woman, as in the extract above
   • the famous Sherlock Holmes
   • Dr Watson, Sherlock Holmes' colleague, who goes with him on all his cases.

2 Decide whether to write in the style of Arthur Conan Doyle, or whether to use a more modern style. Of course, now that Sherlock Holmes is involved, Helen Stoner will be saved from the dreadful fate suffered by her sister. Think of a solution to the mystery and write your story.

Reports of the Martian invasion

These were the headlines which first announced news of the Martian invasion.

DREADFUL CATASTROPHE! LONDON IN DANGER!

In Wellington Street my brother met a couple of sturdy roughs who had just rushed out of Fleet Street with still wet newspapers and staring placards. 'Dreadful catastrophe!' they bawled one to the other down Wellington Street. 'Fighting at Weybridge! Full description! Repulse of the Martians! London in Danger!' He had to give threepence for a copy of that paper.

Then it was, and then only, that he realised something of the full power and terror of these monsters. He learned that they were not merely a handful of small sluggish creatures, but that they were minds swaying vast mechanical bodies; and that they could move swiftly and **smite** with such power that even the mightiest guns could not stand against them.

They were described as 'vast spider-like machines, nearly a hundred feet high, capable of the speed of an express-train, and able to shoot out a beam of intense heat'. Masked batteries, chiefly of field-guns, had been planted in the country about Horsell Common, and especially between the Woking district and London. Five of the machines had been seen moving towards the Thames, and one, by a happy chance, had been destroyed. In the other cases the shells had missed, and the batteries had been at once annihilated by the Heat-Rays. Heavy losses of soldiers were mentioned, but the tone of the despatch was optimistic.

smite – strike

The Martians had been repulsed; they were not invulnerable. They had retreated to their triangle of cylinders again, in the circle about Woking. Signallers with **heliographs** were pushing forward upon them from all sides. Guns were in rapid transit from Windsor, Portsmouth, Aldershot, Woolwich – even from the north; among others, long wire-guns of ninety-five tons from Woolwich. Altogether one hundred and sixteen were in position or being hastily placed, chiefly covering London. Never before in England had there been such a vast or rapid concentration of military material.

Any further cylinders that fell, it was hoped, could be destroyed at once by high explosives, which were being rapidly manufactured and distributed. No doubt, ran the report, the situation was of the strangest and gravest description, but the public was **exhorted** to avoid and discourage panic. No doubt the Martians were strange and terrible in the extreme, but at the outside there could not be more than twenty of them against our millions.

The authorities had reason to suppose, from the size of the cylinders, that at the outside there could not be more than five in each cylinder – fifteen altogether. And one at least was disposed of – perhaps more. The public would be fairly warned of the approach of danger, and elaborate measures were being taken for the protection of the people in the threatened south-western suburbs. And so, with **reiterated** assurances of the safety of London and the ability of the authorities to cope with the difficulty, this **quasi-proclamation** closed.

This was printed in enormous type on paper so fresh that it was still wet, and there had been no time to add a word of comment. It was curious, my brother said, to see how ruthlessly the usual contents of the paper had been hacked and taken out to give this place.

From *The War of the Worlds* by H.G. Wells

heliograph – a signalling device using sun reflected in mirrors
exhorted – strongly urged   **reiterated** – repeated
quasi-proclamation – almost an official announcement

Activities

Reporting facts and opinions

I Read through the passage again, then make two lists.

   a The first list should include all the things **reported as facts** – things which are reported as if they can be proved to be true. For example:

> 'Five of the machines had been seen moving towards the Thames.'

   is an event reported as a **fact**.

   b The second list should include all the things which are **reported as opinions** – comments or statements which people have made but which cannot be proved to be true. For example:

> 'No doubt the Martians were strange and terrible.'

   is an **opinion** expressed by somebody.

Front page news

2 Using the information from this passage, design and write your own newspaper front page spread to break the news of the Martian invasion. Write it as if it were a popular tabloid newspaper reporting these amazing events. You will need to decide on the following:

- a suitable name for your newspaper
- the main headline and some subheadings (subheadings help direct the reader through the report)
- the sort of pictures and captions you will use
- the tone your reports will take (serious, disbelieving, fearful …).

Gulliver's pockets: official report

Gulliver is a prisoner of the tiny Lilliputians. He has been bound and gagged and his belongings have been examined. The extract below is the 'official' Lilliputian report on the contents of his pockets.

In his right waistcoat-pocket, we found a **prodigious** bundle of white thin substances, folded one over another, about the bigness of three men, tied with a strong cable, and marked with black figures; which we humbly conceive to be writings, every letter almost half as large as the palm of our hands. In the left, there was a sort of engine, from the back of which were extended twenty long poles, resembling the **palisados** before your Majesty's Court; wherewith we conjecture the Man-Mountain combs his head, for we did not always trouble him with questions, because we found it a great difficulty to make him understand us … In the smaller pocket on the right side, were several round flat pieces of white and red metal, of different bulk; some of the white, which seemed to be silver, were so large and heavy, that my comrade and I could hardly lift them. In the left pocket were two black pillars irregularly shaped: we could not, without difficulty, reach the top of them as we stood at the bottom of his pocket. One of them was covered, and seemed all of a piece: but at the upper end of the other,

prodigious – extraordinarily large, monstrous   **palisados** – fence of stakes

there appeared a white round substance, about twice the bigness of our heads. Within each of these was enclosed a prodigious plate of steel; which, by our orders, we obliged him to show us because we **apprehended** they might be dangerous engines. He took them out of their cases, and told us, that in his own country his practice was to shave his beard with one of these, and to cut his meat with the other. There were two pockets which we could not enter: these he called his fobs; they were two large slits cut into the top of his middle cover, but squeezed close by the pressure of his belly. Out of the right fob hung a great silver chain, with a wonderful kind of engine at the bottom. We directed him to draw out whatever was at the end of that chain; which appeared to be a globe, half silver, and half of some transparent metal: for on the transparent side we saw certain strange figures circularly drawn, and thought we could touch them, till we found our fingers stopped with that **lucid** substance. He put this engine to our ears, which made an incessant noise like that of a watermill. And we **conjecture** it is either some unknown animal, or the god that he worships: but we are more inclined to the latter opinion, because he assured us (if we understood him right, for he expressed himself very imperfectly), that he seldom did anything without consulting it. He called it his **oracle**, and said it pointed out the time for every action of his life. From the left fob he took out a net almost large enough for a fisherman, but contrived to open and shut like a purse, and served him for the same use: we found therein several **massy** pieces of yellow metal, which if they be of real gold, must be of immense value.

Having thus, in obedience to your Majesty's commands, diligently searched all his pockets, we observed a **girdle** about his waist made of the hide of some prodigious animal; from which, on the left side, hung a sword of the length of five men; and on the right, a bag or pouch divided into two cells, each cell capable of holding three of your Majesty's subjects. In one of these cells were several globes or balls of a

---

apprehended – feared or thought   **lucid** – clear   **conjecture** – guess
oracle – a guide to future action   **massy** – huge   **girdle** – belt

most **ponderous** metal, about the bigness of our heads, and required a strong hand to lift them: the other cell contained a heap of certain black grains, but of no great bulk or weight, for we could hold above fifty of them in the palms of our hands.

This is an exact **inventory** of what we found about the body of the Man-Mountain, who used us with great civility, and due respect to your Majesty's Commission. Signed and sealed on the fourth day of the eighty-ninth moon of your Majesty's auspicious reign.

Clefven Frelock, Marsi Frelock.

From *Gulliver's Travels* by Jonathan Swift

ponderous – heavy   **inventory** – itemised list

Activities

Object identity parade

The report describes at least ten common objects which the Lilliputians have discovered in Gulliver's pockets. The Lilliputians are not familiar with the objects, however, and the description of them, as seen by such tiny people, may make them hard for you to recognise.

I Identify the ten objects found in Gulliver's pockets.

2 For each object select a short quotation from the original description which best reflects the Lilliputian way of describing it.

Your own descriptions

I Select four or five everyday objects and write a description of them from the point of view of a six-inch-high Lilliputian. Remember that they won't be familiar, and you won't be able to name them. Choose items which might be in a pocket or bag, for example:

- mobile phone
- ball-point pen
- cassette tape
- bunch of keys
- lipstick

2 When you have completed your descriptions, get into small groups. Try your descriptions out on each other and see how many can be recognised.

Raising issues

CORPORAL PUNISHMENT

WHAT IS REALLY VALUABLE?

CARING FOR THE BABY

BIG-ENDIANS v. SMALL-ENDIANS

Corporal punishment

This incident takes place at Lowood, Jane Eyre's boarding school. Helen Burns later becomes a friend and inspiration to the young Jane.

'You dirty, disagreeable girl! you have never cleaned your nails this morning!'

Burns made no answer: I wondered at her silence.

'Why,' thought I, 'does she not explain that she could neither clean her nails nor wash her face, as the water was frozen?'

My attention was now called off by Miss Smith desiring me to hold a skein of thread: while she was winding it, she talked to me from time to time, asking whether I had ever been at school before, whether I could mark, stitch, knit, etc; till she dismissed me, I could not pursue my observations on Miss Scatcherd's movements. When I returned to my seat, that lady was just delivering an order, of which I did not catch the import; but Burns immediately left the class, and going into the small inner room where the books were kept, returned in half a minute, carrying in her hand a bundle of twigs tied together at one end. This **ominous** tool she presented to Miss Scatcherd with a respectful curtsey; then she quietly and without being told, unloosed her pinafore, and the teacher instantly

and sharply inflicted on her neck a dozen strokes with the bunch of twigs. Not a tear rose to Burns's eye; and, while I paused from my sewing, because my fingers quivered at this spectacle with a **sentiment** of **unavailing** and **impotent** anger, not a feature of her **pensive** face altered its ordinary expression.

'Hardened girl!' exclaimed Miss Scatcherd; 'nothing can correct you of your **slatternly** habits: carry the rod away.'

Burns obeyed: I looked at her narrowly as she emerged from the book-closet; she was just putting back her handkerchief into her pocket, and the trace of a tear glistened on her thin cheek.

From *Jane Eyre* by Charlotte Brontë

ominous – threatening   **sentiment** – feeling   **unavailing** – useless
impotent – helpless   **pensive** – thoughtful   **slatternly** – sloppy, dirty

Activities

A dozen strokes

1 Make a list of all the ways Charlotte Brontë makes the reader feel that the beating of Helen Burns is wrong. Pick out:

- particular words
- points about the way Helen Burns acts
- points about the way Miss Scatcherd acts
- how Jane's view of the beating affects our views as readers.

Helen's point of view

2 Write Helen Burns' diary entry for that day. She would remember all of the events very clearly, so use the passage to make sure that each one is included. In her diary Helen would be open about:

- how she felt about receiving the beating
- why she acted as she did.

What is *really* valuable?

Robinson Crusoe has been shipwrecked and living on his own on a desert island for more than twenty years. In the following passage he thinks about what is valuable and worth having.

> All I could make use of was all that was valuable. I had enough to eat and to supply my wants, and what was all the rest to me? If I killed more flesh than I could eat, the dog must eat it, or the vermin. If I sowed more corn than I could eat, it must be spoiled. The trees that I cut down were lying to rot on the ground; I could make no more use of them than for fuel, and that I had no occasion for but to **dress** my food.

dress – prepare, cook

In a word, the nature and experience of things dictated to me, upon just reflection, that all the good things of this world are no farther good to us than they are for our use; and that whatever we may heap up indeed to give others, we enjoy just as much as we can use, and no more. The most **covetous, griping** miser in the world would have been cured of the vice of covetousness, if he had been in my case; for I possessed infinitely more than I knew what to do with. I had no room for desire, except it was of things which I had not, and they were but trifles, though indeed of great use to me. I had, as I hinted before, a parcel of money, as well gold as silver, about thirty-six pounds sterling. Alas! there the nasty, sorry, useless stuff lay; I had no manner of business for it; and I often thought with myself, that I would have given a handful of it for a gross of tobacco-pipes, or for a hand-mill to grind my corn; nay, I would have given it all for sixpenny-worth of turnip and carrot seed out of England, or for a handful of peas and beans, and a bottle of ink. As it was, I had not the least advantage by it, or benefit from it; but there it lay in a drawer, and grew mouldy with the damp of the cave in the wet season; and if I had had the drawer full of diamonds, it had been the same case, and they had been of no manner of value to me because of no use.

From *Robinson Crusoe* by Daniel Defoe

covetous – greedy   **griping** – grasping

Activities

Is Robinson Crusoe well off?

1 Discuss the following statements with a partner or a small group.

   a Robinson Crusoe is a rich man.

   b Robinson Crusoe is a poor man.

   c Robinson Crusoe is satisfied with what he has.

   d Robinson Crusoe is foolish not to understand the value of money,

   e Robinson Crusoe understands the real value of things.

2 Which statements do you agree or disagree with? Make notes and explain why.

Message in a bottle

3 As well as learning how to survive on the desert island, Robinson Crusoe has learned something about the true value of objects. He has learnt how to live without using money or giving a monetary value to things. He will want to pass on this understanding to other people in the world, especially as so many seem obsessed with getting more and more money. Since he has no means of direct communication with anyone, Robinson Crusoe will have to send a message in a bottle and hope that it is found by someone.

Write the letter he will send, explaining why he thinks that money is 'nasty, sorry, useless stuff'.

Caring for the baby

Tess Durbeyfield, a young unmarried country woman, has a new baby. In the following passage Thomas Hardy lets the reader understand the difficulties Tess is experiencing.

They went to breakfast, and came again, and the work proceeded as before. As the hour of eleven drew near a person watching her might have noticed that every now and then Tess's glance flitted wistfully to the brow of the hill, though she did not pause in her **sheafing**. On the verge of the hour the heads of a group of children, of ages ranging from six to fourteen, rose over the stubbly **convexity** of the hill.

The face of Tess flushed slightly, but still she did not pause.

The eldest of the comers, a girl who wore a triangular shawl, its corners draggling on the stubble, carried in her arms what at first seemed to be a doll, but proved to be an infant in long clothes. Another brought some lunch. The harvesters ceased working, took their **provisions**, and sat down against one of the shocks. Here they fell to, the men **plying** a stone jar freely, and passing round a cup.

Tess Durbeyfield had been one of the last to suspend her labours. She sat down at the end of the **shock**, her face turned somewhat away from her companions. When she had deposited herself a man in a rabbit-skin cap and with a red handkerchief tucked into his belt, held the cup of ale over the top of the shock for her to drink. But she did not accept his offer. As soon as her lunch was spread she called up the big girl her sister, and took the baby off her, who, glad to be relieved of the burden, went away to the next shock and joined the other children playing there. Tess, with a curiously stealthy yet courageous movement, and with a still rising colour, unfastened her frock and began suckling the child.

sheafing – putting cut corn into bundles (sheaves) **convexity** – rounded top
provisions – food **plying** – passing round
shock – a group of twelve corn-sheaves propped together

The men who sat nearest considerately turned their faces towards the other end of the field, some of them beginning to smoke; one, with absent-minded fondness, regretfully stroking the jar that would no longer yield a stream. All the women but Tess fell into animated talk, and adjusted the disarranged knots of their hair.

When the infant had taken its fill the young mother sat it upright in her lap, and looking into the far distance **dandled** it with a gloomy indifference that was almost dislike; then all of a sudden she fell to violently kissing it some dozens of times, as if she could never leave off, the child crying at the **vehemence** of an onset which strangely combined passionateness with contempt.

'She's fond of that there child, though she mid pretend to hate en, and say she wishes the baby and her too were in the churchyard,' observed the woman in the red petticoat.

From *Tess of the d'Urbervilles* by Thomas Hardy

dandled – bounced up and down on her knee   **vehemence** – force

Activities

Close reading

1 How can we tell that Tess is anxiously waiting for someone or something to arrive?

2 How does Tess set herself apart from the other harvesters at their break?

3 It seems clear that Tess is filled with conflicting feelings about her baby. Look back through the passage and collect evidence to show that Tess at once loves her baby and yet also has feelings of indifference, even dislike. Fill in a chart like the one below, using quotations from the passage.

Evidence that she loves the baby	Evidence that she is unsure of her feelings for her baby
Glance flitted wistfully to the brow of the hill.	Dandled it with gloomy indifference.

A letter to Tess

1 At the break Tess sets herself apart from the other people and does not seem willing to talk to them. What would you say to someone in her situation?
With a partner, discuss:
- the situation Tess is in
- the problems she is experiencing
- advice you might give her.

2 On your own, write your letter of advice to Tess.

Big-Endians v. Small-Endians

This famous piece of writing pokes fun at the ways in which tiny differences can be built up and extended into major conflicts.

The two great Empires of Lilliput and Blefuscu have been engaged in a most obstinate war for six and thirty moons past. It began upon the following occasion. It is allowed on all hands, that the primitive way of breaking eggs before we eat them, was upon the larger end: but his present Majesty's grandfather, while he was a boy, going to eat an egg, and breaking it according to the ancient practice, happened to cut one of his fingers. Whereupon the Emperor his father published an **edict**, commanding all his subjects, upon great penalties, to break the smaller end of their eggs. The people so highly resented this law, that our Histories tell us there have been six rebellions raised on that account; wherein one Emperor lost his life, and another his crown. These civil **commotions** were constantly **fomented** by the monarchs of Blefuscu; and when they were **quelled**, the exiles always fled for refuge to that Empire. It is computed, that eleven thousand persons have, at several

edict – an order proclaimed by a ruler   **commotions** – disturbances
fomented – encouraged   **quelled** – crushed, defeated

times, suffered death, rather than submit to break their eggs at the smaller end. Many hundred large volumes have been published upon this controversy: but the books of the Big-Endians have been long forbidden.

From *Gulliver's Travels* by Jonathan Swift

Activities

Law of the land

I What is the Lilliputian law which is being referred to in this extract from *Gulliver's Travels*?

Petty differences

2 Take a petty difference which others could turn into a matter of absolute life or death. For example:

- left-handers always go first
- people with centre partings get given the best jobs
- only green-eyed people can vote.

With a partner, think of further examples.

3 Take one example and discuss how it could be built up into a law. What sort of measures might be needed to enforce the law? For example, if only green-eyed people could vote there might need to be eye-colour inspectors who would check babies at birth. It might become a crime to wear coloured contact lenses at the time of an election … When you are ready, get into small groups and share your ideas.

Christmas message

4 The conflict between the Small-Endians and Big-Endians has been going on for years. Keep the conflict going even longer by writing the Lilliputian Emperor's Christmas message to the Small-Endians. What would he need to say to boost morale amongst Small-Endians everywhere? He might talk about:

- why the dispute started in the first place
- why the terrible history of last 30 years had been worth all the sacrifice
- why Small-Endism is still so obviously superior to Big-Endism
- why the future clearly belongs to Small-Endians.

Endings

HOW *DID* IT END?

THE DEATH OF THE MARTIAN INVADERS

A FINAL ADIEU

How *did* it end?

This passage describes what happened when, before the eyes of the narrator, the evil Mr Hyde drank a mysterious potion and was transformed into Dr Jekyll.

Mr Hyde put the glass to his lips, and drank at one gulp. A cry followed; he reeled, staggered, clutched at the table and held on, staring with infected eyes, gasping with open mouth; and as I looked, there came, I thought, a change – he seemed to swell – his face became suddenly black, and the features seemed to melt and alter – and the next moment I had sprung to my feet and leaped back against the wall, my arm raised to shield me from that **prodigy**, my mind submerged in terror.

'O God!' I screamed, and 'O God!' again and again; for there before my eyes – pale and shaken, and half fainting, and groping before him with his hands, like a man restored from death – there stood Henry Jekyll!

What he told me in the next hour I cannot bring my mind to set on paper. I saw what I saw, I heard what I heard, and my soul sickened at it; and yet, now when that sight has faded from my eyes, I ask myself if I believe it, and I cannot answer. My life is shaken to its roots; sleep has

prodigy – monster

left me; the deadliest terror sits by me at all hours of the day and night; I feel that my days are numbered, and that I must die; and yet I shall die incredulous. As for the moral **turpitude** that man unveiled to me, even with tears of penitence, I cannot, even in memory, dwell on it without a start of horror. I will say but one thing, Utterson, and that (if you can bring your mind to credit it) will be more than enough. The creature who crept into my house that night was, on Jekyll's own confession, known by the name of Hyde and hunted for in every corner of the land as the murderer of Carew.

From *The Strange Case of Dr Jekyll and Mr Hyde* by Robert Louis Stevenson

turpitude – depravity

Activities

Discussion

1 Look at the first paragraph again. Describe the four stages of the transformation.

2 The story Dr Jekyll tells the narrator seems too dreadful to repeat. Find three examples in the last paragraph of the effect the story has on the narrator.

3 What do you think of the last paragraph? Does it make a satisfactory ending? Discuss your views in a small group.

The moment of transformation

4 In the passage the transformation from Mr Hyde to Dr Jekyll is described in less than a hundred words. It is made to seem urgent and exciting through the choice of words. Write your own description of a transformation in about 150 words.

a You could start in a similar way: 'He put the glass to his lips and drank at one gulp…'

b You could choose another sort of transformation, for example:
  • a human changes into an insect
  • a child changes into an adult
  • a girl changes into a boy.

The death of the Martian invaders

This passage describes, often in quite scientific terms, why the Martian invasion of Earth failed.

I hurried through the red weed that choked St Edmund's Terrace (I waded breast-high across a torrent of water that was rushing down from the waterworks towards the Albert Road), and emerged upon the grass before the rising of the sun. Great mounds had been heaped about the crest of the hill, making a huge **redoubt** of it – it was the final and largest place the Martians had made – and from behind these heaps there rose a thin smoke against the sky. Against the sky-line an eager dog ran and disappeared. The thought that had flashed into my mind grew real, grew credible. I felt no fear, only a wild, trembling exultation, as I ran up the hill towards the motionless monster. Out of the hood hung lank shreds of brown, at which the hungry birds pecked and tore.

redoubt – the innermost refuge in a fortification

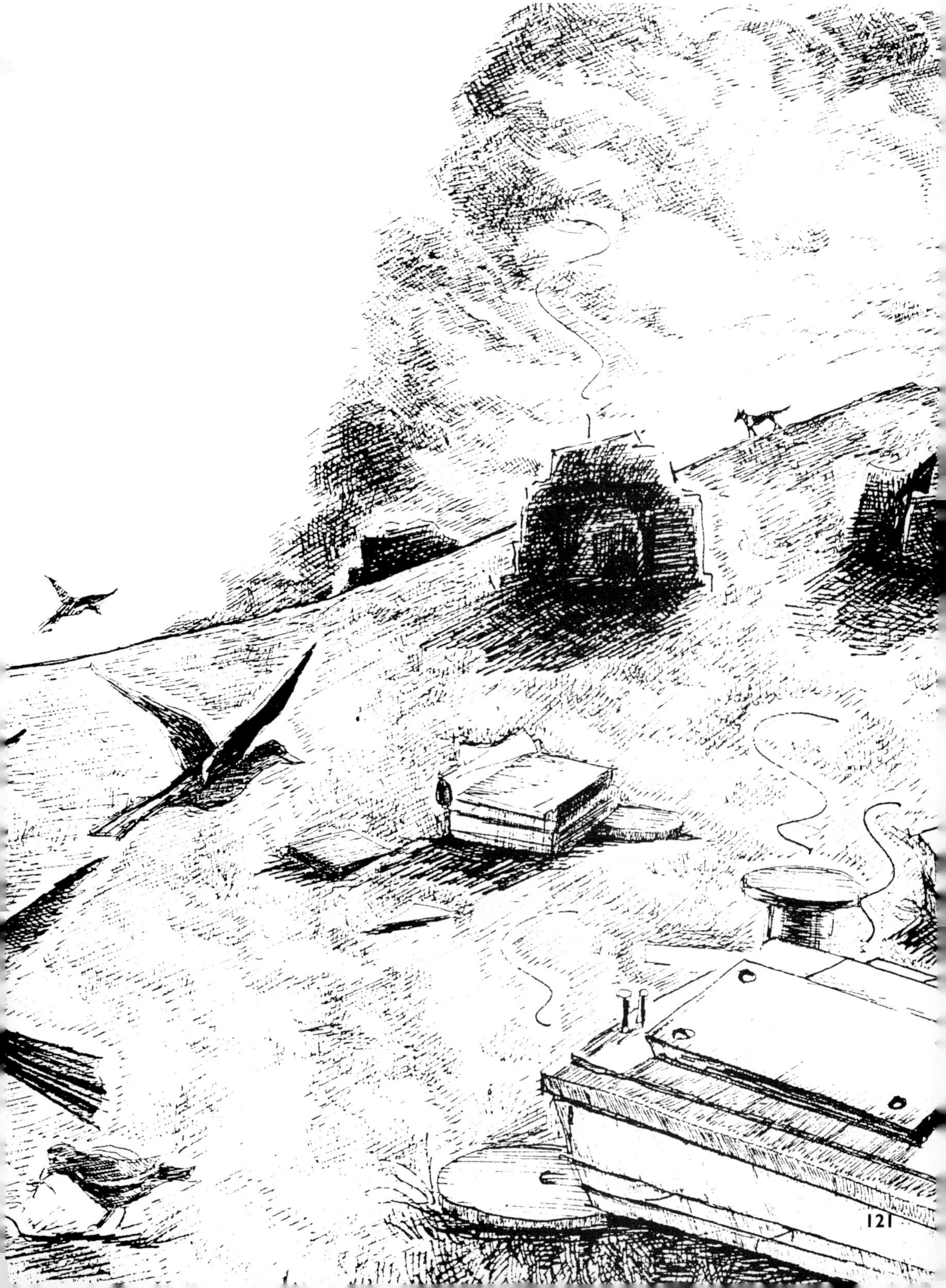

In another moment I had scrambled up the **earthen rampart** and stood upon its crest, and the interior of the redoubt was below me. A mighty space it was, with gigantic machines here and there within it, huge mounds of material and strange shelter-places. And scattered about it, some in their overturned war-machines, some in the now rigid handling-machines, and a dozen of them stark and silent and laid in a row, were the Martians – *dead*! – slain by the **putrefactive** and disease bacteria against which their systems were unprepared; slain as the red weed was being slain; slain, after all man's devices had failed, by the humblest things that God, in his wisdom, has put upon this earth.

For so it had come about, as indeed I and many men might have foreseen had not terror and disaster blinded our minds. These germs of disease have taken toll of humanity since the beginnings of things – taken toll of our prehuman ancestors since life began here. But by virtue of this natural selection of our kind we have developed resisting power; to no germs do we **succumb** without a struggle, and to many – those that cause putrefaction in dead matter, for instance – our living frames are altogether immune. But there are no bacteria in Mars, and directly these invaders arrived, directly they drank and fed, our microscopic allies began to work their overthrow. Already when I watched them they were irrevocably doomed, dying and rotting even as they went to and fro. It was inevitable. By the toll of a billion deaths man has bought his birthright of the earth, and it is his against all comers; it would still be his were the Martians ten times as mighty as they are. For neither do men live nor die in vain.

From *The War of the Worlds* by H.G. Wells

---

earthen rampart – defensive mound of earth   **putrefactive** – causing rotting
succumb – give in

Activities

Why did the Martians fail? What exactly happened?

1 Read through the passage and then get into small groups. Discuss what it was that stopped the Martian invaders from carrying out their mission. Use as much evidence as you can from the passage.

'Man has bought his birthright of the earth'

2 A difficult point is being made in the final paragraph of the passage. Staying in your small groups, discuss what sense you can make of this ending. What do you understand by the last three sentences in particular, starting 'It was inevitable …'?

Magazine feature

3 Write a feature article for a serious magazine for young people. Attempt to:
  - describe what actually happened to the Martians
  - explain why their mission was doomed to failure.

A final adieu

Cathy, Heathcliff's only true love, has died. Heathcliff calls upon Cathy's ghost to haunt him. Although this scene is not the actual ending of the novel (it moves on to tell the story of the next generation), there is a sense of an ending here.

'May she wake in torment!' he cried, with frightful vehemence, stamping his foot, and groaning in a sudden **paroxysm** of ungovernable passion. 'Why, she's a liar to the end! Where is she? Not *there* – not in heaven – not perished – where? Oh! you said you cared nothing for my sufferings! And I pray one prayer – I repeat it till my tongue stiffens – Catherine Earnshaw, may you not rest, as long as I am living! You said I killed you – haunt me then! The murdered *do* haunt their murderers. I believe – I know that ghosts *have* wandered on earth. Be with me always – take any form – drive me mad! only *do* not leave me in this abyss, where I cannot find you! Oh God! it is unutterable! I *cannot* live without my life! I *cannot* live without my soul!'

He dashed his head against the knotted trunk; and, lifting up his eyes, howled, not like a man, but like a savage beast getting goaded to death with knives and spears.

I observed several splashes of blood about the bark of the tree, and his hands and forehead were both stained; probably the scene I witnessed was a repetition of others acted during the night. It hardly moved my compassion – it appalled me; still I felt reluctant to quit him so. But the moment he recollected himself enough to notice me watching, he thundered a command for me to go, and I obeyed. He was beyond my skill to quiet or console!

Mrs Linton's funeral was appointed to take place on the Friday following her decease; and till then her coffin remained uncovered, and strewn with flowers and scented leaves, in the great drawing-room. Linton spent his days and nights there, a sleepless guardian; and – a circumstance concealed from all but me – Heathcliff spent his nights, at least, outside, equally a stranger to repose.

paroxysm – uncontrollable fit

I held no communication with him; still I was conscious of his design to enter, if he could; and on the Tuesday, a little after dark, when my master, from sheer fatigue, had been compelled to retire a couple of hours I went and opened one of the windows, moved by his perseverance to give him a chance of **bestowing on** the fading image of his idol one final adieu.

He did not omit to avail himself of the opportunity, cautiously and briefly; too cautiously to betray his presence by the slightest noise; indeed, I shouldn't have discovered that he had been there, except for the disarrangement of the drapery about the corpse's face, and for observing on the floor a curl of light hair, fastened with a silver thread, which, on examination, I ascertained to have been taken from a locket hung round Catherine's neck. Heathcliff had opened the trinket and cast out its contents, replacing them by a black lock of his own. I twisted the two, and enclosed them together.

※　※　※

The place of Catherine's **interment**, to the surprise of the villagers, was neither in the chapel, under the carved monument of the Lintons, nor yet by the tombs of her own relations, outside. It was dug on a green slope, in a corner of the kirkyard, where the wall is so low that heath and bilberry plants have climbed over it from the moor; and peat mould almost buries it. Her husband lies in the same spot, now; and they have each a simple headstone above, and a plain grey block at their feet, to mark the graves.

From *Wuthering Heights* by Emily Brontë

bestowing on – giving   **interment** – burial

Activities

A film version

Imagine that you are filming this scene. You need to create a detailed shooting script which brings out the finality of Cathy's death and its effect on Heathcliff. Make brief notes about the following:

I The characters

   a Heathcliff – what should he look and sound like? Think about his:

- appearance
- clothing
- features
- accent.

   b Nelly – what should she look like? How should she act in this scene?

   c Edgar Linton – How important is his part? Will he need to speak?

2 The scenes

   a There are four scenes you need to capture:

- Heathcliff by the tree, and Nelly's approach to him
- Edgar Linton and the coffin inside the house
- Heathcliff coming in through the open window and Nelly's actions after this
- the graveyard.

   b Think about how best to use the camera:

- when would you want to use close-ups?
- when would you want to create a sense of distance and space?
- how will you create the sense of time passing?

3 Sound

   What kind of music or sound effects should accompany this scene?

4 Now write your own shooting script. Use the film storyboard on page 90 to show how each scene should be filmed. Introduce your work with some general points about character and location.

About the books

Robinson Crusoe by Daniel Defoe (1719)

Daniel Defoe wrote the story of Robinson Crusoe when he was nearly 60. With its personal style and slow build-up of detail, people have presumed it was based on Defoe's life. In fact he was born and died in London. Although he travelled in Europe, he never went on a long sea voyage. *Robinson Crusoe* was first serialised in the *London Post*.

Gulliver's Travels by Jonathan Swift (1726)

Jonathan Swift was born in Ireland and was later made a Dean at St Patrick's, Dublin. He held strong views on the political questions of his day and wrote many pamphlets on religion, war and the political situation in Ireland. His style was often satirical and ironic, pouring subtle scorn over his opponents' views, sometimes in a darkly humorous way. *Gulliver's Travels* was, and still remains, a great success.

Frankenstein by Mary Shelley (1818)

The idea for this novel came to Mary Shelley during a holiday on Lake Geneva in Switzerland. The Shelley family group amused themselves in the evenings by sharing ghost stories. Mary Shelley's contribution was destined to become one of the most famous.

A Christmas Carol by Charles Dickens (1843)

In December 1843 Charles Dickens was busy writing monthly instalments of his novel *Martin Chuzzlewit*, but he told his friends that he wanted to use his 'odd moments of leisure' to write a story which would show the great hardships faced by poor people, especially poor children. This story was *A Christmas Carol*.

Wuthering Heights by Emily Brontë (1847)

Emily Brontë lived most of her life in Yorkshire with her father, brother, and sisters, Charlotte and Anne. She died of tuberculosis at the age of 30 in 1848. *Wuthering Heights*, her only published novel, received no recognition during her lifetime.

Jane Eyre by Charlotte Brontë (1847)

Charlotte Brontë's novel, *Jane Eyre*, was published in 1847. It immediately received praise and admiration. Charlotte Brontë lived longer than her brother and sisters, and became famous as a writer in her lifetime. She died at the age of 39.

Silas Marner by George Eliot (1861)

George Eliot was the pen name used by Mary Ann Evans who was born near Nuneaton, Warwickshire, in 1819. Mary Evans chose to hide her real identity because she was convinced that her work would not be fully valued if it were known to have been written by a woman.

The Strange Case of Dr Jekyll and Mr Hyde by Robert Louis Stevenson (1886)

Although R.L. Stevenson studied law he was always determined to become a writer. He liked to explore the streets of Edinburgh searching out bizarre people he could use as characters in his stories. *The Strange Case of Dr Jekyll and Mr Hyde* came from a dream Stevenson had, 'a fine bogy tale' which he wrote down as soon as he woke up.

Tess of the d'Urbervilles by Thomas Hardy (1891)

When *Tess of the d'Urbervilles* was published there was a storm of protest about the sympathetic way it dealt with the story of a young woman becoming an unmarried mother. Hardy subtitled the book 'A Pure Woman' and wanted readers not to judge Tess, but to understand her.

The Adventure of the Speckled Band by Arthur Conan Doyle (1891)

Sherlock Holmes is the fictional detective created by Arthur Conan Doyle in 1887. The detective stories featuring Sherlock Holmes and Dr Watson were published in *The Strand* magazine and became enormously popular.

The War of the Worlds by H.G. Wells (1898)

H.G. Wells was a well-known writer on social and political affairs but his novels also reflect his interest in science and technology. *The War of the Worlds* describes the impact of a Martian invasion on Victorian England.